ENCORE

NFSPS ANNUAL CONTEST ANTHOLOGIES

Encore Prize Poems, Editor Kathy Lohrum Cotton
2016 • 2017 • 2018 • 2019 • 2020 • 2021 • 2022

BlackBerryPeach Poetry Prizes, Editor Joseph Cavanaugh
2017 • 2018 • 2019 • 2020 • 2021 • 2022

STEVENS POETRY MANUSCRIPT CONTEST WINNERS

Unpacking for the Journey, Carol Clark Williams
In the High Weeds, Jennifer Hambrick
So Kiss Me, J.W. Coppock
Snake Breaking Medusa Disorder, Flower Conroy
Border Crossing, Amy Schmitz
A Landscape for Loss, Erin Rodoni
Midnight River, Laura Hansen
Beast, Mara Adamitz Scrupe
Breaking Weather, Betsy Hughes
Full Cry, Lisa Ampleman
Good Reason, Jennifer Habel

COLLEGE UNDERGRADUATE POETRY CONTEST WINNERS

Melanin Sun (-) Blind Spots, Danae Younge
Ragweed Body, Intrid Piña
twenty , Josephine Widjaja
Nicodemus, Avreigh Watson
Survival of the Fittest, MeiMei Liu
Sweetwork, Jacie Andrews
The Happening, Deanna Altomara
From the smoking courtyard, Caleb Rosenthal
A Monster the Size of the Sun, Iryna Klishch
Imperial Debris in Quisqueya and Beyond, Catherine Valdez
A Natural Cacophony, Sydney Lo
Exhales, Brian Selkirk
Elegy for Your Eyes, Anna Goodson
But Sometimes I Remember, Michael Welch
Here I Go, Torching, Carlina Duan
The Hole of Everything, Nebraska, Max Seifert

ENCORE

PRIZE POEMS
2022

Editor

Kathy Lohrum Cotton

National Federation of State Poetry Societies, Inc.
nfsps.com

Encore Prize Poems 2022

Published June 2022
National Federation of State Poetry Societies, Inc.
nfsps.com

Edit and design by Kathy Lohrum Cotton
Set in Minion Pro Medium and Myriad Pro Condensed

Cover photo by Luke Stackpoole
NFSPS Medallion, David Nufer Photography
Title with permission of Alice Briley, Past President, NFSPS

ISBN: 9798837020728
Imprint: Independently published

Printed in the United States of America

NFSPS, organized in 1959, now includes more than 3,500 members from 29 state poetry societies. The Federation is a non-profit organization, exclusively educational and literary and dedicated to the furtherance of poetry on the national level. It annually sponsors:

- **Fifty poetry contests** (plus three student contests added in 2020) with cash prizes totaling more than $8,400, including a grand prize of $1,000, plus publication of each contest's top-three winning poems in the annual *Encore Prize Poems* anthology.

- **The Stevens Poetry Manuscript Competition** for a single author's collection of poems, with a cash prize of $1,000, plus publication and 50 copies of the book.

- **The College Undergraduate Poetry (CUP) Competition** with two awards, the Meudt Memorial and Kahn Memorial, each offering a $500 prize, plus chapbook publication, 75 copies, and convention travel stipends.

- **The BlackBerryPeach Poetry Prizes for Written and Spoken Word Poetry,** which blends "stage and page," awarding three prizes, totaling $1,750, plus chapbook publication and copies, performance video posting on YouTube, and first-place convention travel stipends.

- **The Manningham Trust Student Poetry Contest,** which includes a junior division for grades 6–8 and senior division for grades 9–12. The top ten poems in each division at state-level competitions advance to the national contest. The top ten national winners in each division receive cash prizes and publication in the *Manningham Trust Poetry Student Award Anthology*.

- **A national poetry convention**, hosted by a member state society, with poetry workshops, speakers, panel discussions, presentation of awards to contest winners, open-mic readings, and entertainment. The first hybrid convention was hosted in Ohio and virtually in 2022.

For further information, visit nfsps.com.

CONTENTS

CONTENTS

CONTENTS

Encore 2022 brings to print the prize-winning poems read to attendees at our first-ever hybrid convention, held in June both virtually and at Columbus, Ohio. In this anthology are the top 159 prize poems, chosen from more than 6,000 submissions, with 187 international entries from countries including the United Kingdom, Spain, Mexico, Canada, India, Ukraine and Czechia.

Again added to our traditional 50 annual competitions are three student categories. Awards for high school, middle-school and grade-school poets are offered without entry fees.

Readers will find wide variety in this volume, with fixed poetry forms such as pantoum, villanelle, golden shovel, rondeau, haibun and sonnet added to free verse, prose poems, cento and others. Contest themes are also wide-ranging: the geography of fire, loss of a child, listening, daily rituals, the sea, and dozens more.

Each contest's subject or form is listed above the poem so you can share some beginning points for their inspirations and challenges. Find more details for each contest in the Contests: Sponsors, Guidelines & Prizes listing (pp. 204–207).

Lou Jones opens our 2022 edition of *Encore* with the three-page, $1,000 prize-winner, "Ginsberg," while youth from across the nation close the collection. Between those pages lie sorrow and humor, wisdom and passion, and the uniqueness of many voices, styles and interpretations. We invite you to explore the anthology's diversity, cover-to-cover.

We also welcome you to learn more about the National Federation of State Poetry Societies and our 29 member state societies, across the country from California to New York; Minnesota to Texas. Note the lists of our contests, publications and leadership, and for more information visit nfsps.com. Thanks for supporting poets and poetry by reading this year's NFSPS anthology.

Kathy Lohrum Cotton, Editor
June 2022

1st Place, Lou Jones, Pooler GA

Ginsberg

I saw the best minds of my generation destroyed by madness,
starving hysterical naked, dragging themselves through the
negro streets at dawn looking for an angry fix….

Thus Allen Ginsberg opens his magnum opus, *Howl*,
heralded as one of the great literary achievements of
the 20th century, acclaimed for its unrestrained style and
dismissal of the academic literati—a lamentation on
failings of post World War II society, a tempo-allegro
"first thought, best thought" catalog of people and places,
art and music, sex and drugs, a syncopated chorus of sanctimony,
dissolution and despair, amplified by crescendos of
language-frenzy, elegiacally toned, consecrated within
the canon of artistic works of the era, a manifesto of dissent
that stoked the Beat movement, an "emotional time bomb"
Ginsberg foresaw capturing the consciousness of
future generations should the military-industrial complex
evolve into an authoritarian state—a narrative in
free verse that stands with Kerouac's *On the Road* and
Burrough's *Naked Lunch* in the treasury of *Beat* literature,
a work first staged by Ginsberg at San Francisco's *Six Gallery*
in the presence of bohemian devotees who cheered
in cultish unity as the timid scholar, poet prophet,
planetary thinker, burned through the verses, incanting
line after line, jolting the senses with the exploits of the
Beat minions, those "best minds" of his generation who
expressed rebellion through their licentious behaviors.

Many believed "best minds" would have been best
characterized as "troubled minds," a small cadre on
the East and West Coasts, poets and writers, artists and
musicians, radicals and communists, *true believers*
in search of an identity, with a need to belong, vanguards of

a new culture, living in a blur of illusion, impulsivity, and
collective thinking, forswearing a productive life to the appeal of
the counterculture, a generation unto themselves, cast as
exploited and repressed, their inability to assimilate driven by
society's bourgeois mores—*Beats* seen as self-indulgent,
vulgar, brazen and reckless, whose rush of deviance travels
faster than the mind's ability to grasp without a breath to
settle one's thinking, angry voices condemning the values of
a capitalist country seen as destroying the lives of artists, writers,
the creative and sensitive, whose aspirations were frustrated by
a culture of materialism and enlightened self-interest, young
"outcasts" spurned by a citizenry unmoved by their intellectual
righteousness, spiritual piety, and carnal excesses, expressed through
a moveable bacchanal of narcotics and alcohol, promiscuity and
personal risk, the lifestyle of those on the margins, junkies,
vagabonds, idlers and thieves, "angelheaded hipsters," embracing
precarious credos and promises of ecstasy through Utopian
stateliness—the *Beats*, Ginsberg's core group of literary
mavericks, philosophers, and the mystically advanced,
whose motivations clashed with the convictions, ambitions, and
intellectual reach of the best minds of society at large.

Nowhere in Ginsberg's condemnation of an unjust America
can be found words such as purpose and decency,
accountability and self-respect, initiative and ambition,
wisdom and grace. Were the *Beats* spoiled shirkers who
blamed society for the futility of their lives, who in their
self-pitying abdication were captured by their own choices,
who exhibited little in their conduct that might evoke admiration,
accord, or empathy? The excesses of Ginsberg and his disciples
came at a high cost, behavior-ignited "madness" that "purgatoried"
many in a world of drugs, visions and "waking nightmares."
In time the *Beat* movement gave way to the 60s *flower power*
communal platform of anti-war activism.

Was Ginsberg proud of his life and the quest for
transcendence in a broken world, a belief that
the most saintly among us are those who express their humanity
through the magic of the arts and higher states of consciousness—
did he and his congregation of acolytes make a difference,
did their rejection of a conformist society nudge it toward
an awakening, have lives of the disenfranchised improved,
is the country more just, considerate and tolerant,
would Ginsberg be encouraged, celebrate today's activism as
aligned with a vision of the freshened planet he craved—
would his "best minds" feel more liberated in the America of today,
enjoy greater artistic freedom, be less prone to self-destructive behavior—
how might Ginsberg have retooled the machinery of the nation,
would his prescriptions for cultural rebirth have considered
the realities of man's differing expectations and motivations—
did he believe mankind could be redeemed, that society could
advance an Elysian setting for the aesthetically advanced,
that new versions of humanity were thinkable?

Allen Ginsberg is among the 20th century's most
celebrated writers, who, with his iconoclastic literary brethren,
expanded the boundaries of literature forever. He attacked
the culture for its spiritual dearth, bigotry, and avarice, even as
he capitalized on that culture. In time he softened toward
"Moloch whose blood is running money," the metaphorical
god of capitalism he so despised and feared. Ironically,
his outrage against a materialistic America became
a lucrative undertaking—
    Irwin Allen Ginsberg died a multimillionaire.

2nd Place, Martha H. Balph, Millville UT

Pandemic Year 2020: A Haiku Journal
(haiku sequence)

microscopic wisp
of protoplasm forces
the world to its knees

cruise ships quarantined
for weeks—thousands now dying
of cabin fever

hand sanitizer
and face masks gone—even worse,
no toilet paper!

Italy locked down—
yet from every balcony
arias take flight

carbon emissions
globally reduced—thanks to
coronavirus

alone and dying
on the far side of the moon—
those in ICUs

less fragile by far
than humankind's tangled world—
an orb-weaver's web

coronavirus—
unknown to the meadowlark
who sings in my field

in the ICU
mourning is prohibited—
tears could spread virus

social distancing—
first-world privilege, perhaps?
what of Africa?

urban dwellers lived
without birdsong, without stars
until—pandemic

as with pandemic
so with climate change—those who
cause least, suffer most

George Floyd lies dying—
COVID victims lie dying—
their cry: I—can't—breathe!

20-20 world
appears to lack clear vision—
still the sun rises

birdsong and wordsong—
twin beacons of sanity
in a viral world

gathered in a tree
by the COVID patient's home—
a murder of crows

answer the doorbell
to greet a Halloween spook—
coronavirus

clatter of dead leaves
beneath October blue moon—
skeletons dancing

we are mask-weary—
so much weight in wariness—
COVID year wears thin

3rd Place, Budd Powell Mahan, Dallas TX

Beyond Words

I struggle to arrange a plane of phrase
and write a documentary, a page
that marches in, a verbal polonaise
that reenacts as surely as a stage.
Yet somehow my vocabulary fails.
The words lie flat unable to convey
the great intensity, the subject pales
in alphabet's infinity of gray.
The one dimension of the printed sheet
inks lines to conjure back reality.
Inherent is a whisper of deceit
for tiers that syntax cannot make one see.

The reader masters every document,
creating shadows of the work's intent.

I read of Sandy Hook, the Holocaust,
the beach at Iwo Jima's scarlet tide,
and find emotions stirred are quickly lost.
I was not there, it was not I who died.
Though haunted, I can never really know
the wound of loss, the agony they wrote
into the starving days, the truncheon's blow,
the noose upon the final pulse of throat.
I would not suffer, yet I am bereft
that what I know is not an absolute
but mere interpretation. I am left
with only constructs fact cannot refute.

A sentence may evoke facsimile,
the mind's creation of reality.

The limitations of the pen and tongue,
present the hurdles writers often vault.
The script is written, every passage strung
with truth and fact, each chosen letter wrought
to write the wrong, the beautiful, the dark.
The poet finds each word, the perfect choice
to bring a moment delicate and stark
a declaration in unequaled voice.
The breath of life is paragraphed and blown
into each braided, forged, and sculpted rhyme
and once released the crafter stands alone
begins again in what remains of time.

What vein of truth is pierced by reader's eye,
exsanguinates to leave the writer dry.

Constellations

after "All the Love You've Got" by Carl Phillips

In the evening, after folding the children
into their beds as she wishes she could fold

the stars into the sky—that same gentle
containment, and the faith in it, because she is

mother here, which means folding, at least
outwardly, every wandering hand and loose

strand of hair—she has now returned
to the kitchen, where the evening must be.

There's the window, holding out the wild,
as windows must do. And outside, the meadow,

holding up the sky. And in the meadow,
a woman. The mother presses against the glass.

The woman wildly but carefully rises and twirls,
trailing her fingers through the air, over and over

again, as if weaving an invisible basket.
Dancing? Chasing? She's too grown to chase,

thinks the mother, who can't help noticing how
the woman brings a faint elegance to her pursuit—

an elegance some might confuse for gathering. But
the mother knows gathering, which is to say,

she recognizes unruliness when she sees it.
What does elegance have to do with gathering?

What do windows have to do with folding?
The mother knows she should leave

the woman alone; she isn't harming anyone.
But still she opens the door, steps into the yard.

The sky is dark but not altogether dark
and the meadow breathes softly with life.

The mother presses forward. Beneath her
checkered skirt, each fold neatly pressed,

her feet swish through the grass. And as
she passes deeper into the night—

which, by this time, has somehow become
both one with the meadow and nothing at all—

pinpricks of stars begin to rise like wildness
itself from its depths. The lights tickle and swirl

as they glide past her skin. The mother laughs
and spins to catch them on her fingertips.

How easily the lines unravel between fireflies
and sky. How small the window suddenly appears.

2nd Place, Laura Altshul, New Haven CT

Fledgling

In the heat, the open window beckons.
Her family napping in the tenement apartment.
She creeps to the ledge,
sits on the sill, her sturdy young body
anchored to the stone. Dangles
her legs from the third-story perch.
So still, no breeze. From inside,
the faint whine of fans moving hot air.

The sky, studded with birds,
white gulls flying languidly, and she flaps
her wings, shuts her eyes,
flies off with them, rising, rising—
streets, buildings, trees shrink
to blurs of gray and brown and green
and space grown large, endless, cool.

Curved yellow beak beside her,
dirtied feathered wings
so close no longer white but grayed—
black eye staring. She is with
this bird, her winged arms
beating in rhythm with avian stealth.

Pulled down by strong hands
that grasp her bare shoulders
and yank her back into the room's heat.
I flew with the birds, the girl cries
as her mother sobs and hugs and slaps.
Why did you stop me? I flew, I flew.

The Insufficiencies of Mirrors

"Sometimes it's easier to look through
a window than into a mirror," he said
watching Paul sit quietly down.
"The problem with a mirror is that it
doesn't give you a way out—it reflects
what is seen. Sometimes it doesn't look
familiar. You know. I sometimes say,
'Is that me I'm seein'?'" He waits for Paul
to reply. Silence. Raises his head, says
to the bartender, "Another, please." She
pours a beer, acts as if he's the only
one at the bar. "Paul," he says softly,
"when I look out I can see what can
be out ahead of me. Feel something
pullin' on me. Feel I might be free
from who I've been, free to be who I
am to be." Sees Paul slipping away
slowly. "We all have the right not to be
who we've been!" he says loudly.
The bartender turns. Raises her eyebrows
in a question. "Not yet," he says. "Doesn't
that make sense? And maybe a mirror is to
remind us we need a window to look out
of. Something ahead to pull us through."
He sighs. "A short one, please," he says
as if he's been asked a question. She brings
the beer, asks, "Who you talking to?" He
looks at the mirror behind the bar,
the window by the door. Doesn't reply.

1st Place, Cheryl Van Beek, Wesley Chapel FL

Instars

She presses seeds she got from school into the earth.
When the first set of true leaves stretch out their arms,
she knows they've rooted.
Parsley decorates the garden like paper lace.
She picks the leaves for recipes.

One morning she cringes—
black worms crawling on her herbs.
She picks them off.
Fennel perfumes her fingers with licorice.
Ferny fronds of dill tickle her wrist.
Her hands relish the scent of pickling cucumbers
like a butterfly tasting with its feet.

Next morning, the worms return, devouring the leaves.
She picks them off again, but day after day
they come back, growing bigger, leaving only stripped stems.
Each day she stares at the bare stalks.
Then one rainy morning, lime-green
fortune cookies hang from silk threads.

A chrysalis clinging to a branch, becomes clear—
inside, a folded note.
A swallowtail butterfly slits its envelope.
Black and yellow wings open like a parachute,
flutter to dry, and shake off the past.

Years later, through job loss, break-ups, grief,
she remembers that first pinprick of shiver.
Though she never saw the tiny butterfly eggs,
their message seeded inside her—
the gold embryo of faith.

What if the many-footed creatures
that come to us cloaked,
that strip away our leaves and gnaw at our roots,
what if all our cocoons, and worm-like phases
are just caterpillar stages—instars
on a path we can't see all at once
that unfolds with each turn of the kaleidoscope?

2nd Place, Melissa Huff, Champaign IL

Riverspeak

after Veronica Patterson

First, I must speak of whispering my troubles to the stones,
their churning foam washing away my agitation.

But I also speak of whatever the water whispers to me—
the rippling tongue of its movements, the cadence
of its currents, teaching me to flow unfettered.

I speak of the conversation between us—the river's
speech as it spills into my veins, soothes my pulses, how its
language swells, subsides, its murmurings echoing my own.

I will let the rivers speak their own names—Roaring Fork,
Big Sandy, Brandywine, Cascade, Whitewater, Blue Earth,
Stillwater, Wind.

All of this speaks something about the comfort of constant
changefulness, slipstreams running past quiet pools,
the calm embedded in forward motion.

3rd Place, Susan Chambers, Mankato MN

Sustenance

When a father drowns himself in the quarry
it feels as bad as the tribe felt when
reindeer stopped flowing north.
Grandfather used to say,
"The secret of happiness is balancing
between remembering and forgetting.
Forgetting loses nothing; to forget is
to be reborn." I think he died, then.
I worry about the quarry's depth.
Will such a waterlogged site
hold bones for nine thousand years?
Will strangers be able to tell
from father's skeleton about his habits:
how he ate apple muffins over the sink
at six in the morning, how his work clothes
hung on the hook at the door?
I want to sink into language, go to the store,
teach school, put a derby on my head.
"How do you learn to not recall?"
I want to ask Grandfather.
I could forget by beginning to drink,
heavily and openly, but I always
find myself when I get sober.
I do not know if father drank last night.
He has four children, each with a different mother.
But I think he was mostly moral.
I know he thought reindeer were important.
He kept antlers, hide, teeth, even hooves
on his homemade oak shelves in our floral living room.
"They are the source of all materials

we ever need" he said. "We can depend on them entirely."
Almost every Saturday father drinks, faithful
as the old courthouse clock. I saw the Sheriff's car
coming down the gravel road through the heavy sleet.

I said, "something's wrong, isn't it?"

I said, "hell of a time to go swimming."

1st Place, Janet Ruth, Corrales NM

Trick of Light

Golden Shovel from lines by Eva Saulitis,
"Prayer 45," *Prayer in Wind*

Sit with me beneath the fading stars, take
a sip of life—both bitter and sweet—embrace this
contradiction as an antidote for the insistence
of summer sun and uncertainty. Listen to ticks of
night insects chanting unfathomable questions. Birds
sing the monotonous refrain without the answers. And,
with starry red flowers and hairy leaves, a galaxy of weeds
muscles up in inconvenient places, an invasion certain to
take over our ambivalent lives. These interruptions mean
that life burgeons, full of confidence and fecund, and death's
her twin sister, clasping what they know between them. The
waves of our uncertainty ebb and flow, but always the mind's
digging for truth down some obscure and dusty cul-de-sac
in the maze of mysteries, looking for tangibles; while
outside, in the ever-expanding universe, death claps as life
rides a comet's tail across the Milky Way. Knowledge is

un-knowing.   Gaining more means knowing less, a
cipher for which we have only a partial code, a trick
of science and spirit, a black hole inhales the certainty of
all we cling to in our blindness, loosens our grasp at light.
But in the vortex of darkness, above the howling, there is a
whisper—age-old wondering, an aching desire, a persistence
seeks what we do not know. The cosmos exhales a breath of
dark matter and stardust, murmurs secrets on a solar breeze,
engulfs us in the wind of un-knowing, while sneaking
with us, a peek at what we suspect lies beneath.
Someone hands us a rough stick or smooth pebble, the
tool with which we can prop up the sagging sash
on the window of not knowing. The ancient wisdom of
those who came before, painted on rocky walls inside the

cave with spirals, hand prints, and animal spirits—the old
ones, who leave cobwebs draped across the dingy window
of our minds. The sticky strands let in just a bit of light that
allows us to see the way along dark corridors, but it will
cast shadows across our knowing. We can see we are not
gods, yet in our ignorance, the window is not fully shut.

Stars & Earth, Straddling Worlds

Golden Shovel poem après Billy Collins

Awake in the dark— / so that is how rain sounds / on a magnolia.
—Billy Collins, *She Was Just Seventeen, Haiku*

The Tibetan plateau is always awake,
a living escarpment in
the bony spine of the
Himalayas. Skies, limpid and dark—
whisper to prayer flags flapping in high passes. Thin air so
raw and biting, even with summer sun, that
ice rimes every tuft of grass. Each blade is
thick with brightness. I can see how
time expands. Heavenly bodies rain
a billion pinpoints of light. Blue sounds
of mountains echo a living voice. Ghostly images on
Milky-Way-wooly clouds are a
shaggy yak, creamy-pink as buds of kisopa magnolia.

3rd Place, Christine Irving, Denton TX

The More Things Change…

Not under foreign skies
Nor under foreign wings protected—
There, where misfortune had abandoned us.
        –Anna Akhmatova, "Requiem"
        (Born 1889, Ukraine; died 1996, Russia)

We wake to chaos, our daughter between us, not
suddenly shredded in the upstairs nursery under
a roof exploded in the night by foreign
guns. Outside, we kneel beneath threatening skies
Nothing can dim our gratitude. Neither bombs nor
armies weigh against the safety of our child. Under
the stars, we pray to every god we know, both foreign
and familiar, to root us deep in love, send wings
to carry us through separation, keep our child protected.

Loving baby, loving country, he must fight and I
must carry her to safety, everything we've shared
at risk. Broken bridges, beleaguered battlements, all
spell disaster. We resist while the world watches this
story replay across its screens. Nations have toyed with
fire before and burned and yet, even knowing better, my
mind justifies, defies, demands retaliation, claims to own
the high ground. As if that ever made dead people
rise again and live. I cannot abide for long there
in that place of right and wrong, no answers dwell where
only mind inquires. Love's the way to thwart misfortune.
Exponentially, multiplies itself. All the loving I've had
remains inside, integrated in flesh, never to be abandoned.
Thus, we are seen and known; never alone, forever—us.

1st Place, Cathryn Essinger, Troy OH

Letter to My Congressman

Two a.m., and the dog is pawing at the bed again
alerting us to thunder some place in the Midwest,

or fireworks over St. Louis, or someone pointing
weapons at defenseless animals in the name of sport.

No lesson in logic or geography will settle him
until I get up to tidy the kitchen and read

the computer news, while he shelters under
the table on top of my feet. I read about threats

that he does not understand—viruses, conspiracies,
people held hostage by their own ignorance, and

since I'm up, I decide to write to my congressman,
who invites concerned citizens to leave emails

that he will never return. I begin: "I am a concerned
citizen with a restless dog." I run my bare foot across

the dog's wide back, ruffling and smoothing his fur,
assuring him that I have not forgotten his concerns

about fireworks and guns, and officials whose manners
are so appalling they are practically asking to be bit.

I should go back to bed soon, but I don't want to lose
my momentum as I lay down one sharp sentence

after another, retreat, rewrite, substitute anger
for conscience and think better of it, nor do I want

the calming reason of dawn, the familiarity of
routine, or anything that will keep me from

explaining that I am a citizen with a dog whose
head now lies so heavy on my feet that I know

he will soon be immune to all of the human fears
that are going to keep me awake all night.

House of Bears
after photographs by Dmitry Kokh

From a camera drone, the running
buzz of tiny propellers draws
them out from weary windows
and busted-out door frames of

a long-abandoned weather station
on Kolyuchin Island in the Chukchi Sea.
This fabular nest for polar bears,
looks like an eerie movie set

with its rickety front porch
and weathered walls.
Raisin eyes and plush-toy snouts
pose for the logic of their curiosity

and the showy illusion
of their translucent fur.
I imagine ACTION!
and then it's the scraping

of claws over warped floorboards,
shortwave static from phantom
radio channels, ghosts of brewed
coffee and boisterous laughter.

Do these Arctic creatures take turns gnawing
on a forgotten broomstick to clean their
incisors, lumber to corners of the house as
it teeters from side to side, rumble around

empty oil barrels in the yard so
the ventricles of their hearts fill
with joy? I linger on these photos
through the night, my gaze longing

as their dark eyes gaze back. A milky
sun rises on an overcast morning
as the bears wander through
this deserted building on a rocky shore.

They will hunt, swim among the ice
floes, survive stormy winds and rain
and the fog that will push up against
their warm haunches, until it doesn't.

Music Swash & Backwash

The ocean doesn't need a five-line staff
to anchor tunes. A chambered shell
collects bone-curled notes
dropped by dying waves. Listen.
Press the nautilus to your ear. Hear water
molecules boiling in nebulas—a fermata

in space time. Rolling waves hesitate in fermata,
collapse over pockets of air. Endless variations staff
the sea's sway. Rowdy water
crests tumble, ebb in pools of blue. Heaven's shell
pouts with envy. Gray swells pause, listen
for distant obbligato, notes

anxious for a whipping wind. The oceanologist notes
a calm sea—sardine schools in silver fermata,
a fertile crescent. Overhead, pelicans listen
to undercurrents, plunge through the staff
of their life. Clamped beaks shell
blue sheath, scoop fish from water.

Satisfied, they skim off, leave water
awash in feathered debris & jumbled notes,
a toccata out of fugue. Stars, shell
foils in night sky, tremble pianissimo, no fermata
stays their burning. Perhaps a staff
of fanciful angels stokes the fires. Listen

as they siren songs into the void. Listen
to music of the spheres, water
flooding from black holes beyond Earth's staff.
Only fish with lateral notions sense the notes.
Bottom plodders in semi-fermata,
they adopt each drop. One oyster shell

swaddles a grain of sand. Shell
& grain rough it out for years, listen
for a pearl stalled in perfect fermata.
Frederick Handel composed *Water
Music* for a float up the Thames. Notes
stumbled off the deck. King George & staff

sat in the shell of the royal barge as tide water
propelled them to Chelsea. Listen for those notes,
babbling in waterlogged fermata, buoyed by a cheeky staff.

1st Place, Elaine Zimmerman, Hamden CT

Blue Parrots Watched

The cicadas hum thick and familiar,
like a recurring dream. Repeating
an endless yearning, from the trees.

Where did you go that night when
the dancing ebbed? The two-step
slow and silky. On the veranda,

a few sang. Bourbon and laughter
turning in circles. Blue parrots
watched from a gold-painted cage.

Someone toasted an occasion; but
then a tin noise of nothing shook
the Spanish moss. Let's be clear.

No one expected blossoms so late
in summer. Just a whiff of fragrance
and dew. Magnolias lit up the hillside

like opal moons. Some petals already
falling; the edges frayed and burned
from the sun's sluggish stare.

2nd Place, Janet Watson, Wesley Chapel FL

Redneck Boys

Where summer was impossibly long and steamy,
boys grew up to be tougher than alligators,
and they often liked to prove it.

More than once I witnessed their primal
manhood stunt of dropping down
from a low-lying branch onto the backs
of sleeping gators in the tannin-dark shallows
of our backwoods creek, then run across
those knobby hides, awakening
primordial grouchiness and barely escaping
savage teeth and slashing tails.
Sweat-soaked when they reached the bank,
they'd forget to laugh in victory
when the gators grew tall on their fat legs
and lumped after them. The boys
always outran the monsters, but terror
told me there was great possibility that
one day they might not.

Today I was cold-soaked, walking a dark street
in Atlanta rain. Passing between brick walls,
far from the gator swamp of my rural youth,
I heard a huffing, smelled a predator.
Years and miles narrowed. Gripped
by terror, I recalled the boys—
how fast they ran. The beast behind me
drew closer and I didn't have to look to know
that hungry eyes were shining in the gloom.
This southern girl knows how to run
as though my life depends on it.
I learned that from redneck boys.

3rd Place, Cheryl Van Beek, Wesley Chapel FL

Florida Love Bugs

Maybe they take to heart
Aristophanes' myth,
that to be whole you must
find your other half.
Magnets pulling
in opposite directions

they attract
bonding back to back.
In Florida, twice a year
their swirling black clouds swarm the air.

They resemble fireflies
minus the fire.
They walk up your arm
faint as fading dreams.
Sunlit thoraxes
a shower of carnelian beads.

Thread legs, seamed black stocking wings
ready to tear at the lightest touch,
point outward like ballet slippers
in first position.

After a few weeks,
they drift apart.
One lies on its side,
front legs curled up
as if it were a cat napping.

Its partner enjambs itself
over both sides of the doorbell,
its legs like backward handlebars.
Wings open like scissors,
even in death it clings.

1st Place, Anita M. Krotz, Salt Lake City UT

The Bread Platter

Family memories grow from deep loam. Nonna is as jeweled as iridescent peacock plumage. Her accent, chiseled from foothills of the Italian Alps, makes air around her seem enchanted. She learns early to be creative— painting, poetry, pottery from Great Grandpa Nonno Carlo—sewing, baking, cursive writing from Great Grandma Nonna Maria. Afternoons, Nonna's voice floats over me like musical notes, falling into her native tongue as she teaches me thoughts are things. We draw and bake together. She says art soothes the soul with satisfaction, and food feeds body and spirit As I grow, she says, the easel will help me escape madness and the kitchen, melancholy. Those parts I don't understand yet. She is gone now, but still with me when I teach my own granddaughter to push away chaos while she paints, to hold off craziness when she captures poems. Tuesday afternoons we make Nonna's three ingredient loaf of bread, crusty outside, soft inside, just like some people. It cools on her homemade platter, crazed with age. I hope the dish survives another generation, an homage to cherished grandmothers' love.

2nd Place, Janet Watson, Wesley Chapel FL

Garam Masala

I blend spices until they become the egg-yolk color
of monks' robes. Cumin, cinnamon, cardamom, clove,
nutmeg, ginger, and tamarind, fennel seeds, mustard
seeds, mace and star anise, saffron, garlic, turmeric,
bay, coriander, crushed malabar leaves, and a punch
of chili pepper heat will warm the body and sweeten
the tongue.

Into the simmer of meat or fish or lentils, I will stir a
slight spoonful of this spicy muddle—right at the end,
providing a fragrant finish to what we will eat. Dinner
guests will consume more than food. They will step
into a voluptuous panorama of great gray elephants
and jungled green, marble temples and diamond peaks
reclining against the bosom of a sapphire sky, and
women in saris, bright as butterflies, their silver ankle
bracelets jingling as they shop in the market for melons
and marigolds, for ginger, saffron and malabar leaves.

Oh Hunger

Oh hunger! Why do you know my name so well? You
call with fried chicken and ham, with yeast rolls and white
rice, with potatoes prepared in every way imaginable, with
barbeque and carrot cake and bagels smeared with a thick
comforter of cream cheese, with gumbo, jambalaya,
etouffee, and boudin, with pies and elotes dripping with
fresh drawn butter and lemon pepper, with black-and-white
cookies and baked brisket, and gefilte fish and lox and apple
strudel, with Chinese dumplings and Korean dim sum, with
burgers and hot dogs and buckets of popcorn drowned in butter.
Oh hunger, sweet hunger, in the name of Saint Julia Child,
please learn someone else's name.

1st Place, Jerri Hardesty, Brierfield, AL

Litany for Robin

Depression is a steel trap.
Depression chews off the clamped limb,
But still does not allow escape.
Depression is a vacuum,
It is a black hole
That even light cannot break itself out of.

Depression is not a lack of intent.
It is not a selfish retreat.
Depression is not just a bootstrap pull
Away from defeat.

Depression is a crusher of hope.
It has a weight and a will of its own
That can prevent all other
Free will from blooming.

Depression is a vicious circle
That just keeps spinning down.
Depression thrives on gravity.

Depression is not simple.
It has no secret remedy,
No formula of alchemy
To turn things back to gold.

Depression is a thug,
A thief in the night,
An abusive demon song
That lodges in the eardrum
Until there is no other
Sound.

Eagle Omens

The birds of prey threaten to circle my life
until I stop the path I'm on and start a new one.
I wend through my days. I do not look for them
yet they happily appear, one after another.

The first explodes upwards from a deer carcass
in the highway. He drips entrails,
a bright crimson wound against
the purity of white head feathers.
I violently swerve,
pull my car onto the crunchy gravel shoulder,
watch warily as he returns,
drifts on silent wings
back down to the bloody body.
He rips once more at dead flesh.

The second eagle floats
on lazy air currents above the river.
I am positioned at the meeting table,
my eyes are drawn to her again and again
as she searches from a lofty vantage point.
She sees a different path from her height
as she glides past my window.
With a mystic's vision she points to a different road
than I drove this morning when I left the warmth of my bed,
had to swerve to avoid her brethren.

The last of the eagles come to me this spring.
A camera placed high in a tulip tree
on the other side of the country,
allows me to watch them emerge from two eggs.
Small, covered with grey fuzz, they open, tiny grasping beaks,

beg for strips of fish torn from bones by talons curved and sharp.
The disclaimer at the bottom of the screen reads;
"this is a wild eagle's nest, nature can be disturbing,
watch at your own risk."
Sibling rivalry does not become an issue for this pair,
they do not push each other from their shelter.
Instead, by late summer they dive from the edge,
spread massive brown wings and seek a place to call their own.

dark army

They invade overnight, silently, while I sleep in my bed. Hundreds, thousands of them. Little black ants stream in across the floors, climb up the cabinets in a dark column of urgency and fan out on the kitchen counters. They grab what little spoils are left there from last night's dinner.

This army of ants is industrious and persistent despite the warm wet sponge sweeping up dozens of them and flushing them down to a watery grave. Confounded they race around trying to regain their secret-scented path.

Sometimes it is not food that these tiny bandits are after. Sometimes they are just thirsty from a dry spell during the winter months. I wish I could have a non-lethal barrier that keeps the ants outside my home. Instead, I...

Trace the long line
back to its source and
offer sweet poison.

1st Place, Cheryl Van Beek, Wesley Chapel FL

Woodwinds

Sun crosses its arms over the timberland, a fortress of light it weaves,
with pipe-cleaner branches of feather-needled leaves.
It beams through triangular crowns to divine
ringed secrets, ages spiraled in hearts of pine.
Inside their trunks, treasure of resin
seals and heals wounds—vaults of medicine.
A tidal wave of pine trees dance,
hypnotize with swaying chants.
I follow trunk shadows that stripe the grassy pike
like straps of a giant's boot marking the hike.
Forest bathing cleanses my senses. I walk through an arboreal haiku.
Here, there's no need for defenses. Japanese call it "shinrin-yoku."
Green-dipped branches paint the sky's canvas of chalcedony.
The boiling kettle voice of wind hosts a green tea ceremony.
I join the ritual,
free myself from all habitual.
Bursts of pine needle-rain remind me: the woods speaks in poems,
feel each step, savor the earth's haibuns and evergreen Oms.

Matsukaze, the Japanese word for wind through pine trees
wind-milled mantra, the call and response of needles and breeze.
Voices reedy—then low, shift pitch as winds blow.
Needles quiver and shimmer, swift—then slow.
Wind whips through pine, blowing rhymes.
Conifers answer in rippling chimes.
Wind's sibilant roar tingles, draws me like a hidden spring,
invisible sage hushes through pines whispering.
Beyond the balsam scent, in knots deep inside,
beneath cracked bark, ghosts of old branches hide.
Knots in my stomach unwind in sun-tinseled glow,
swept away by pine warblers' yellow trill, presto.

Ache of sunset's fading blush,
despite tidings of dusk, I don't rush.
Whiskbroom tassels bristle my wrist. Leaves crackle,
startle a chipmunk munching bark.
I curl my fingers around this moment, shadowed by the creeping dark.
The end of another day—my urge to cling swells into a tsunami.
Wind whooshes, folds it into tomorrow's origami.

2nd Place, Christine Irving, Denton TX

Forest

Bud, leaf, twig, stem,
branch, bark, cambium,
trunk, root, sap, cone,
heartwood, xylem, needle, phloem,
forest, stand-of-trees, bosque,
woodland, grove, orchard, copse,
greenwood, primal lung of earth,
rain-soaked sponge in summer's dearth,
shelter, shield, apothecary,
cathedral, windbreak, sanctuary.

3rd Place, Russell Strauss, Memphis TN

Toward Mississippi Pines

The slightest splash of turpentine
stirs my memories of pine.
I am traveling South,
refugee from elm and oak
over blacktop roads toward home and folk
near the Tallahatchie's mouth.

Shortleaf and loblolly green
will defy the browning wintry scene.
In wind these trees, unbroken,
will sway like courtiers in dance
who in stiff but amorous circumstance,
bow to beaux bespoken.

Rooted in Mississippi loam,
my kin call the evergreens their home,
standing pine-firm, by God's grace,
in a land where resin sates the air
and the nuthatches nesting pair by pair
bless their coniferous sacred space.

1st Place, Budd Powell Mahan, Dallas TX

Blue Bouquet

Your gloves lie caked with mud atop the gate,
where in the quitting hour they were draped,
and there they wait for hands that won't return.
Within the hour, fate had claimed a prize,
the garden wilted in survivor's guilt,
and bees paid honor, drank the salty damp
arranged in indigo upon the fence.
What sacrilege would cause me to remove
these artifacts that mark a final day?
The fingers flower like a final grace.
And so you speak again in rusty hinge,
the cairn you left upon the weathered board
arranged in contours of the flesh and bone
once held and kissed and lifted in a prayer.
The winter soon will fill the rose's beds,
and night will find the bloom atop the stave
divinely white, a color to concede
a judgment to the solstice of the spring.
In April breeze enlaced in digits grip
the lilacs will embrace all raveled hems.

2nd Place, Lorrie Wolfe, Windsor CO

Yellow Swallowtail

After a year of gray veils,
clutching my loneliness like a rosary
rubbed smooth and familiar,

today a yellow swallowtail
lights on the milkweed
that has, at last, bloomed its pink fist open,
a pale planet bobbing atop a thin green tower.

I have for years cut down this juicy stem,
thinking it an invasive weed
among my purple salvia,
till a green-thumbed friend
described its magnetic effect on the butterflies.

I let it grow.
And this year
a giant flutter, a flit of butter-gold
filigreed with black lacework
alights and flexes.

The wings pulse...pulse,
a rhythm matching my heartbeat.
Silently it moves from blossom
to blossom, sipping life.

I barely breathe, lest it disappear.
Could anything be more alive
in this moment?

Yellow glow brings me home to mid-summer,
to rippling heat, a joy so full
there is no room for yesterday's grieving here.
        Today, I make a choice—to praise.

Emerging from sorrow's cocoon,
I re-enter the world
of beating sun, milkweed, and butterfly,
each of us awakened,
our new wings testing the wind.

flowerbed, south exposure

faded flowers nod
hot breezes buffet small moths
toads dislike dry air

sweet, hidden nectar
marauding bees delve for gold
scorching sun roasts all

long drought saps color
hot wind riffles through dry leaves
stressed, they turn early

leggy, bleached zinnias
ragged butterflies stop, rest
flowerbeds, havens

tattered, parched, and scorched
gardens wither into fall—
hummingbirds fly south

late autumn boughs dip
wind presages winter
golden leaves drop, spent

1st Place, Patricia H. O'Brien, Old Saubrook CT

Disconnected

after Peter Halley's *Rectangular Prison with Smokestack*, 1987

Excerpt from an interview with Professor Craig Haney on
"Fresh Air," March 6, 2014: *I remember talking to a prisoner
in Massachusetts who explained to me that he had a practice
that he was very proud of, and he described in great detail how
he disassembled his television set and ate the contents of it and
then was taken to a....*

The man-high wheel
of withered roots
and sodden earth,
unequal match
for this winter's
wind and ice,
looms taller now
than the felled tree's
heft and once   majestic   height

even as

the man
in his solitary cell,
hunkered over
his TV, dismantles
and ingests
dial/ wire/
staple/screw
then waits
for the guard who'll try
to stand him up   to walk him

somewhere.

2nd Place, Kathy Lohrum Cotton, Anna IL

The Workman

after *Steel* from *America Today*
by Thomas Hart Benson, 1930

In these post-war days of raw hands
stoking the smoking flame, spilling
the mill's red-gold molten streams,
the workman is steel-hard—muscled
arms bared to sleeveless undershirt,
heavy shoes edging flame. He is a sweaty
cog in the great noisy wheel that turns
time and the nation.

Nearby, a foreman, hands clasped behind
his back, oversees the clamorous work
from a wall's high edge. He cannot
imagine a future where robotic arms
replace aching flesh, where the workmen
with empty pockets are a forgotten gear
in the machinery of obsolescence—a word
they will learn only by the cold touch of it,
all rust and fleck and deafening silence.

3rd Place, Martha H. Balph, Millville UT

Adam's Hand

On the discovery of 30,000-year-old
rock paintings at Chauvet Cave, 1995

In what Pleistocene night
did he dare
with human eyes

to steal
from rhinoceros, from owl,
from hyena,

from saber-toothed tiger
primordial power?
In the forbidden cave

of my ancestor's dream
shall I remember
how to read

cursives of horn,
hoof, and tusk?
On these sacred walls

dare I apprehend
secrets
encoded in feral eyes?

Will the bear's white skull
so perfectly centered
on a black rock

roar anew
the dreaded oracle?
Behold

on a far wall
the blurred silhouette
of four fingers

and a thumb:
the father's hand,
my own.

1st Place, Lisa Toth Salinas, Spring TX

On Getting the House After the Failed Marriage

A Cento

You can't deny the inspiring pathos of ruins,
the beauty of endings,
and how powerful it is, this breaking off.
Or so I tell myself my darkest days.

This is the world we wanted.
That place I ran from, now
like the resurrection.
Like sanctuary, or second chances,
a house to re-build & re-burn. Not to be confused with rage,
not in the way a night can swarm to flame,
where the blind stirring of love becomes a sharp dart.

Here is where I cry alone.
Let us call it home. Let us call it a city,
a field where want
conceived out of nowhere
is in pieces—shattered or broken, we say.
At what point is something gone completely?

In the yellow kitchen, a silent anxiety attack,
its little thorns pricking.
Each spring's a wound before it is a birth.

Here in my house whose sunny rooms
hope-against-hope to believe,
I am listening to the echo of my own words,
their dark folds and long list of alternate endings.
"This is plenty." I write, "This is enough."

Sources: 1. Wislawa Szymborska, "Hatred" (translated by Claire Cavanaugh & Stanislaw Baranczak); 2. Christine Valters Painter, "God Among the Pots and Pans"; 3. Maryann Corbett, "The Grandchild of Immigrants Learns a Little Italian";

4. Angela Alaimo O'Donnell, "Flannery's Laugh"; 5. Louise Glück, "Gretel in Darkness"; 6. Jane McCafferty, "What Binds Me"; 7. Felicia Mitchell, "Bristlecone Pine"; 8. Judith Valente, "A Place Called Trouble"; 9. John Sibley Williams, "Origin of Topography"; 10. Melissa Studdard, "Killing the Moth"; 11. Tyler Farrell, "Mystical Daydreaming at the Autumn Faculty Meeting"; 12. Jerry Harp, "Ergo"; 13. Bruce Bond, "Górecki"; 14. Kelly Grace Thomas, "Almost Forty"; 15. David Whyte, "Sometimes"; 16. Sean Thomas Dougherty, "Poem with a Line from Kundera"; 17. Mary Szbist, "The Troubadours, Etc."; 18. Libby Burton, "A Brief History of Hysteria"; 19. Anya Krugovoy Silver, "A Briar"; 20. Sally Thomas, "Holy Week"; 21. Rhina P. Espaillat, "Choices"; 22. Marjorie Maddox, "Seek and Ye..."; 23. Lois Roma-Deeley, "Etcetera Lives"; 24. Nicholas Samaras, "Afterlife"; 25. Daniel Sundahl, "Where Logic Breaks Down."

2nd Place, Crystie Cook, Sandy UT

Retracing Steps to Silence

More than sheer mileage, it was leaves
free-falling which separated us—
no winds of change, only the blindness
of autumn's bluster, caught blowing
through the jumble of college classes.
Or perhaps buildings rose up in blockades
across a campus full of thatched pines,
pontificating professors, serious study sessions.
Early snow silenced the ache of empty arms,
covered the memory of footprints left
by you walking away to board an airplane,
for a two-year mission of working, waiting.
Icy shadows slide across slick sidewalks.
Even the sun turns cold and distant,
wary as a coyote or lone, wild wolf
perched on a flint-thin ridge.
Time scurries away to find squirrels
squabbling over a cache of nuts,
realizing nothing can be saved for winter,
watching as the hollow tree splinters to separate,
derelict and deserted, the way footprints
vanish under waves of seawater
while lone coyotes call...and call...and call.

Dried In

After a few hundred construction woes,
the windows arrive.
They go wobbly in our hands
when the mountains play tricks
with wind that twists
like God's breath in a tunnel.
Once attached, they still tremble
as if they're getting
a talking to.

It's been an eight month wait.
Every beam and stud's capacity for noise
is silenced by the restraint of hammers
and saws. Inside, only insulated quiet
echoes its emptiness.
The recently finished roof has ceased
its commentary. It no longer regrets
the loss of shingles that flew on gusts
toward a valley,
whistling in notes
of receding C minor.

This evening, a door will close
on the last vulnerable space
that lets in a storm.
Rain will have to seek
a destination elsewhere,
having left enough mud on the floor.
In carved teak and burnished brown,
hinged and heavy,
this steadfast wood
will guard all we walk into.
The goodwill at its threshold
will know, with dry feet,
that it is time to come home.

1st Place, Bonnie Anderson, St. George UT

Standing on Two Feet
Remembering my daughter

She dresses herself every morning
with flip-flops and backward socks

Plaid shorts   pockets inside out
skinned knees   silly grin

She stands in front of me waiting approval
raised eyebrows and a smile

Gently tuck pockets in   zip zipper
button buttons   with a hug

She found scissors in my sewing basket
cut her hair into wild-blown dandelion tufts

She wants pigtails today   she'll do it herself
one tail going north   another going south.

She sits for breakfast like a little jewel
silver spoon in hand   Lucky Charms in her bowl

She is ready for the day   no matter how it comes
runs to greet her friends

They all keep time to the same drum
flip-flops   backward socks   hems inside out

Warm Honey and Daggers

The trouble with words is they arrive one
at a time. Choices must be made, nuance
navigated. They appear as through a glass darkly—
in the writer's pen, the speaker's mouth—
and are sent out into the world as if stumbling
through roiling fog, picked up on radar as small,
glowing smudges and trails on a screen,
      signifying nothing—

or too much—They can land
on the ear like a knockout blow
or a tender caress. They settle
sweetly in the heart like warm honey
on the tongue or find their mark
with a dagger's strike. The trouble
with words is their awesome power
      and their pitiful impotence—

their laser aim to wound, their bumbling
attempts to heal. *I take that back,* we say,
knowing there is no White-Out, no backspace key,
no magic eraser, no refunds, no returns. And yet—
they are what we have, what we keep,
what we give—*I love you very much for all time,*
the last words of my beloved to me—
      I wouldn't trade them for the world.

3rd Place, Sheila Tingley Moore, San Antonio TX

Planning Ahead

We're settling in for our weekly card game
and commenting on Sara's new very short "do."
Tact has never been Mary's strong suit,
or suppression, but honesty is, so she asks
Sara why she did it 'cause she liked the old
"do" of a pulled-back bun better.
Kathy and I exchange looks like two
deer caught in Mary's vegetable garden.

*I was afraid the mortuary wouldn't be able
to fix it so I'd look my best—I need a little
fluff around my face if I'm lying down.*

Incredulity and concern joined hands
with panic, but you don't just blurt out
Are you dying? Instead, genius that I am,
I asked *Are you planning on leaving
in the near future?*

It seems she just believes in being prepared.

1st Place, Michael Spears, Plain City UT

Ode to the Iris Bloom

You are a poem of loveliness, unfurling flower,
budding in the May-time hour of my heart's desire.
Your lips, full-blossomed, with delicate kiss elude
the rose's briered glory of blissful solitude.

Such alluring mood persuades the bees to your
delicious delicacies. Arriving in swarms, they relish
your ambrosial charms. In sweet repose, their
dainty anther posed, gathering in your sensual glory.

Hesiod knew the ancients reveled around rainbow
sheaves teething infants on tender tether of earthy
rhizomes, succulently sleeved; exalting in rich
treasures of your faultless feminine pleasures.

I have heard the whispering wings the emerald throated
hummingbird brings while drinking up your nectared wine.
Your heart freely melds with mine in flirtatious fantasy,
filling my woodland gardens with fragrant ecstasy.

I have seen the luster of your emerald shards paying
homage to the sun, the moon, and chatoyant stars
down shining on gaily jeweled gems, bathed in ruffled
robes of leisure on regaled flowing hems.

I have found you wild and wading where mountain streams
have flowed, fish playing at your feet; where the modest
boreal toad finds refuge in the forest of your reeds,
dreaming of hibemacula among tufted, sheltering meads.

I have sensed the fullness of your evolved geometry;
inhaled amorous scent as you sway in tune with a lovely
morning breeze. Such supple compliment of sublimity
must bid a toll. Transcendent flower, you fill my soul!

"Breaking the Rules" note: Interior line rhyme has been used to vary
and maximize the rhythm.

2nd Place, Lorrie Wolfe, Windsor CO

How Women Go Mad

Wyoming is the state with the highest suicide rate, at 29.6 suicides per 100,000 individuals. Medical professionals blame the wind.

I can't think about that right now. If I do, I'll go crazy.
          –Scarlett O'Hara in *Gone with the Wind* by Margaret Mitchell

This banshee wind, will it never stop?
There's nothing out here to break it.
It blows away my every thought.
Just how long can a person take it?

Out here on the plains, nothing will break it
with its endless whoosh and roar.
It shakes me but I can't shake it.
Now it's uprooted the cottonwood, laid it across my front door.

It blows away my every thought,
torn up and wrenched with whoosh and roar.
I too am disjointed, though rest and sleep I've sought,
like the ruckled cottonwood, downed and blocking my front door

This wild wind brings terror and bluster.
I am disjointed from the peace I've sought.
My teeth taste of grit and dust, and what's more,
my hat's a wind-blown bag, and like it, I'm caught.

Branches and root-ball, exposed like dark petticoats.
Wind bellows, every thought escaping,
And that eerie, sudden silence between gusts—
There is madness in that waiting.

          Oh this damned wind—   will it never   stop?

"Breaking the Rules" note: Pantoum with an extra end line.

Disco Ball

If we're not supposed to dance / Why all this music?
          –Gregory Orr, "To Be Alive"

The answer spins from your question, Mr. Orr,
speeds our feet, quickens heartbeats, as *if*
you've tapped a subsurface throb *we're*
all driven by. It's a primal resonance *not*
unlike a ringing bell or tuning fork, *supposed*
to arouse a harmonic bebop *to*
the perpetual pulse of our life's *dance.*

We step to poems and breathe to songs. *Why*
else enfold us in these thrumming senses? Wherefore *all*
these wheeling spiderwebs and falcons? Why *this*
galactic whirl of stars, these rainbows of tulips and *music*
of falling water, and whispery winds in red canyons?

"Breaking the Rules" note: A Golden Shovel poem with an additional first line ending with the poet's name and an additional last line ending with the question mark.

Yellow Sunflowers Against Blue Sky

Last summer, volunteer sunflowers
overtopped the six-foot board fence
along one edge of our yard.

The big, yellow-rayed disks had blue
sky for background—sky the deep, unflecked
blue of summer-long drought.

Sucking nectar from the dozens
of tiny florets composing each disk, bees
picked up pollen from one, shed it on another.

When the pollinated flowerheads
grew heavy with seeds, chickadees
pecked them from their calices.

Last summer, yellow sunflowers
against blue sky were simply
yellow sunflowers against blue sky.

If volunteer sunflowers sprout
this year, and the plants again grow
seven feet tall, lifting their massive blooms

against blue summer sky, they will be
something other than themselves, something
human-drawn borders and humans' brutal

battles for territory have made them:
an emblem of one people in their stand
against another. So humans once enlisted

even roses, setting the red
against the white, calling their human wars
Wars of the Roses. Oh, leave

the flowers out of it! Let
the flowers be
simply themselves.

2nd Place, Lorrie Wolfe, Windsor CO

Borderlines: It's Not About You

...Borderline Personality Disorder is one of the most difficult to treat.
  –Diagnostic and Statistical Manual of Mental Disorders, Fifth Edition

Sheet lightning scalds the sky,
quick and gone.
I should know by now,
in this parched borderland between us
the prospect of rain is a false promise.

Thunder's slammed door enervates
and heat waves rise from the chasms you carve.
Like this storm with its empty clanging.
the lies you spew are mirages—
true only in your own mind.

You are the cracked molar's dry socket,
the blood clot pulled loose
leaving extraction's raw hole—
a dull ache where the root used to live.
        But this is not a poem about you.

It's not about how your absence is a relief
to those who love you
but can't live with you   and live.

This is about how seared blood cools,
the memory of lightning pales,
the fractaled sky finds calm.

This is about how one dawn, I look up
to find there is no storm coming.

This is about how
August's swelter eases into September,
and the bitten edge where love broke off
has worn strangely familiar,
though the tongue still haunts the hollow space.

This is about how blood runs deep,
but also flows away.
This is a poem about how a sere land survives.
This is a poem about how I carry on.

Conversing over Couscous

Our tour guide waved an admonishing finger
tasked to keep idealistic Americans safe
wafting us with smoke of submissiveness
we in his city, the Zanzibar to our Chicago,
the guide knew nothing
proving biases invade borders
I *could* speak the language,
refusing to drink from the chalice,
wishing to connect beyond carpet sellers.

My father-in-law born in Lahore, now Pakistan,
his was not a doubting nature, Papa-ji loved me
fiercely, his American daughter,
the solid scarlet magenta of our bond
a fire as warming as midday light,
he and I islands in a world of division,
unified in our belief of goodness,
goodness common to mankind,
kindness I carted in my backpack.

I stepped off the tour bus,
away from purveyors of argan oil,
disappearing down an alley
of date-laden carts, opening doors
to friendship with total strangers,
conversing over chicken and couscous,
vegetables and spices, in our mixed dish
of languages: shared discourse,
packing my bag chock-full of stories.

I spent a brazen evening on the arm
of a woman whose eyes peered

through a rectangle of blue-black cloth,
we waded through a throng
of brown-eyed babies and cast-offs,
admiring minarets and soaring
architecture, building bridges
with citizens of this land
not so far from home.

1st Place, Terry Miller, Richmond TX

Lon Chaney

Lon Chaney was the child of deaf parents. He changed world cinema by introducing the makeup art to films. He was also regarded as one of the world's greatest character actors.

mother and father, I will pantomime for you
instead of signing—will fashion my face
and protract my posture to make you laugh
to make you cry   to have you understand
what a world of sound is like—what it is
to speak back to the cacophony with image
and pity

I will have a son who I've taken from the wolves
I will be the world's phantom   it's hunchback
whipped for the crime of deformity   I will be
hypnotist and Fagan   will make women faint
and children scream   then they'll come back
to have me do it again

when I'm no longer pleased with whom I am
I'll fashion putty and paint and straggled
clumps of hair to become someone new
to fear or love

even though most of my films will be lost
to the absurdity of time—I will heal and be healed
by my thousand faces   will give everything to cinema
and the long dark silence of my unmarked grave

2nd Place, Jane Kretchmann, Piqua OH

Christine de Pisan Writes to Her Granddaughter

Dearest, I write for you to know the truth
as I approach my inevitable death.
Men will charge I have written only one document
since I entered this convent eleven years ago,
my poem celebrating Jeanne d'Arc. Fadoodle!

Of course they would acknowledge this work,
for it suits their opinion of a subject to which an aging
woman in Christian seclusion should turn her mind.
Yes, the Maid of Orléans possessed strength and virtue,
as did all the women in my *City of Ladies*.

But how could I, who have written every week
since I was widowed so young, turning to my pen
to support myself and my children, neglect my need
to put on paper views that no one else will air?

The old prioress burned my bundle of poems
that pictured nuns in positions of power, replacing
corrupt or weak men who serve France poorly.
Haply, our new prioress supports my writing.

My enemies' spies stole my screed warning of the
insanity of King Charles, which led to my country's loss
at Agincourt. I grieve to hear of the English domination.

No, we are not ignorant of the forces contending outside
these walls. We pray six times daily for the restoration
of the whole of France to the leadership of her rightful
king, grandson of The Wise, of whom I wrote at length,
by commission. But prayers and chores in no way
satisfy my spirit as do hours at my table writing.

Remember these words, my beloved, when others say
I forsook my worldly craft. Let the world know the truth.

3rd Place, Jo-Anne Rowley, Lafayette, CO

In Retrospect
(Voice of Richard Feynman, 1918–1988)

From the beginning I knew.
I, Professor of Theoretical Physics,
spent the days consumed with schemes
of gravity, logarithms, and the like.
Endless calculations written on a rolling board.
On Saturdays I drove from Los Alamos to Albuquerque
to the hospital where you were treated for TB.

The emergency arrived.
Equations left unexplained on a dusty board
I took the quickest route.

When you died, the little clock I gave you stopped.
The clock was delicate and had often stopped in the past.
Through the years I had to keep it going time to time.
Now it stopped again at the very moment that you died.
I sat with you a while and wondered
should I start the clock again?

On the drive back to Los Alamos I fixed a tire
that went flat and all the time I worried
what to tell my friends.
"She's dead" I blurted out
"and how's the project going?"

Five months later in Oak Ridge,
walking past a shop with dresses in the window
I saw a dress you would have liked.
I cried then, Arlene.
I cried for you
and I could not stop.

Whispers

Someone once told me
that the world only speaks
in whispers, so I lean in
real close to hear her.
"I'm listening," I say,
but she holds a blue-sky
fingertip to my lips.
I taste the sun
and feel myself
come undone.

The world only speaks
in whispers, so I stare
at her mouth and try
to thumb through
my layers. Tattered
and jaded, an archive
faded by years
of insecurity
I'm trying to trade
for a sense of tranquility.

The world only speaks
in whispers, and I've learned
she never repeats herself,
so I stand at attention
in the subway station.
I'm tangled in a crowd,
trying to find the silence
in the loud.
Above it all, I hear her
hushed call when she says
to me, finally

"Child, sometimes you have to stand alone on midnight avenues
and let the quiet be something that happens to you."

2nd Place, Terry Miller, Richmond TX

the distraction

after viewing *Death Listens* (1897) by Hugo Simberg,
Finnish National Gallery: Ateneum, Helsinki

as long as the boy plays his violin
his mother lives—death listens intently

each time the visitor starts to turn, the youth
finds another burst of magnetic melancholy
within the strings and his fingers

to hold the boney figure transfixed
in auditory awe—a skinless thumb
to the naked jaw—skull bowed as though
in worship   in prayer

while the boy plays he weeps as he recalls
his mother's humming when she bakes bread
how she holds him close when bedroom shutters
argue with night wind

it is in this way she lives forever
and the boy plays his instrument forever
and death stops for all on a snowy day
in Finland

3rd Place, Christine Irving, Denton TX

Listening for What the Walls Might Say

I shelter in the shade of a simple city stanchion
scrubbed clean of spray paint. No hidden
messages embedded in graffiti's clamor,
no angry chorus of complaints
or self-asserting signatures intrude.

Not long ago, the luster of their neon tweets
made living possible, built a kind of harmony
from chaos, a frame that offered common ground.
In times of scarcity and want, feral children
clutch at any succor the city offers. Hold it tight.
Join. Clasp. Serve whatever cause bestows some sense
of family, camaraderie or care. We trust false gods
and all the tender sounding prophets
who write their names on subway walls.

It got me through, till I clawed out and fell
from bitter want into a better life. No one
could be more thankful.

In a minute, I will walk me home
and eat a mound of chicken
served afterwards with ice cream—
like a scoop of love.

Leaning against this pillar, failing to fully fathom
the weave of fragile happenstance, I listen
for what the walls might say. And though
I can't help smiling at sweet fortune's turn, I wonder
if those vanished urban day-glow scribblings
are yet quite done with prophesy and me?

1st Place, Shari Crane Fox, Grass Valley, CA

Taking off Billy Collins' Clothes
after Billy Collins   –for Emily

You will want to know
that he was standing in the kitchen
near my espresso machine,
      his pupils dilated, and
the slight turn-down of the
left comer of his mouth that he does
when he's excited.

The buckle of a man's belt
is not a place to underestimate.

I moved my hands, one
against his stomach,
the other, lifting the shaft
of his belt buckle loose of the leather
to pull it through
      each loop
of his tweed trousers, and then slowly—
the zipper, his skin beneath marble-
pale and the central
zephyr, firm
like ripe pepper.

Later, at a poetry reading
I described it like climbing a tiny pine,
my legs around the trunk,
but of course, I did not admit everything—
how he dropped
      his pen
to the floor when I grabbed him,
the way he lifted his chin

as he nearly finished, the way he begged
to stay as I pushed him away, yelling
   This one's for Emily!
  as I shoved
  him out my door,
the ensuing silence overlaid
by the buzz of his words from the other side of my thick
oak door,
words like a windowpane tapped by flies, like a
loaded gun
that looks right through you
with one sorry eye.

Unworthy

Otto Schultz loved marble and granite;
made pilgrimages to cemeteries.
He entered by many complaining
gates to study the life of stones.

Why be concerned about the dead?
They are buried deep,
just memories soon forgotten
by Grandpa Johan and Baby Hanna.
Sight of shapely grave markers: black or grey,
was the only thing his mind embraced.
Brown and yellow lichens—age spots
of stones—were continents on his map.
Death dates gave him pleasure,
to know when it was carved.
It was so reassuring to lick
his finger on old sandy grains.

In this place of reflection, he did not
hear the cuckoo call in the beech tree;
did not see blue cornflowers bloom
or smell the surprise of the boasting breeze.
The nightingale of love did not sing
long in his married life; was quickly
replaced by the chirping sparrow of habit.

Inge, his round-shouldered wife, shook her head,
watched him eat the peach of life,
not tasting sweet flesh and nectar;
always settling for the certainty of hard seed.
His death was like rain on her wilting plain.

She opened all the doors in her house,
wore unmatched socks, low cut dirndls.
She wrote poetry and savored good Riesling.

For Otto's last resting place,
she chose a stoneless spot;
gave him a GPS designation.

Spellbound

When the witch cast a spell, she bound the reckless
sex offender to a plate. A bit tighter than she meant,
he lost 30 pounds. Her mixed signals stick and bind.
She sends the crying fool to the seal's cove. Wraps
despair with a hopping rabbit. Roots mania in street tar.

Wish for a lover, find a donkey in the backyard.
Take a lover, he acts more like a donkey than the one
you feed oats to at dawn. (You've taken to the critter.)
Pray for a younger body, find a dream full of toddlers.
Glue rhyme to the crisp sleeve of the dull orator.

A breeze opens to a family eating dinner. Three children
stare. One pets a kitten. The parakeet looks up; drops
caraway seeds from a corner cage. Though no one leaned
forward, candles are blown out; soft wind stills the flicker.
What force keeps the dog, curtain, child hiding behind?

Did the bird sense the cat? Would he fly out if the cage
door blew open? Did she wish for stops or starts? Familiar
like a painting, or a story told again and again late at night.
A small girl laughs; knows more than her strapped red
sandals and small bowl of stars intend to share or shine.

1st Place, Cade Huie, Grand Prairie TX

Scintillation

My cupped hand dips night water
from the pool where fish are sleeping
to become the stuff of stars,
reflections shimmering,
fingers like comet tails, stitching
sky-sequins together in silver nets
where fires lie captive, immersed.

The pond reposes,
silent but for insect chatter,
frog talk, wind whisperings
of missives in dark letters
passed from star to star,
from wing to wing, waiting
for the regal moon's arising.

Light trembles in my shallow palm,
sinks in my skin, its kindred,
before my fingers part to release
glittering drops back into
the mystery from whence they came.

Sitting by the Lake at Chattanooga

Like those that followed men of yore,
a shadow falls from maple limb
and sways as if it hears the hymn
once sprightly sung by marching corps
who now befriend the seraphim.

Reflections kiss the lake and pray
in ripples of concentric waves,
like banners flowing near those graves
where bodies lie, there, blue and grey,
this quiet place our country saves.

I cannot say I know just one
who rests among these small white stones
and yet I hear their baritone's
sure tone, and frozen grip on gun,
their brows deep furrowed by unknowns.

So here I sit, within this scene,
where sunlight sparks across the lake
and, at attention, egrets stake
their post beside the rolling green,
as if to honor, not forsake,
each brave and battered soldier-soul
who lies within the honor roll.

At Chattanooga we extol
their sacrifice and toll.

3rd Place, Julie Kim Shavin, Fountain CO

Pentaprism

Art is not a reflection of reality, it is the reality of a reflection.
                                        –Jean-Luc Godard

That everyone here will become everyone here
is not open to discussion, merely denial.

Reflections of skyscrapers reflect skyscrapers,
and nothing is anything if not infinitude.

Out the car window, white nomads of sky
quicken and swim, building to building.

Your eyes confound with all the redoubling, tripling.
New things will be said of the ancient heavens,

all cobbled from former philosophies, and even you,
vanished, will leave some double behind you.

1st Place, Kathy Lohrum Cotton, Anna IL

Because You Choose Me

It's like you've won the playground
coin toss, and the league champ is
a ringer for your team, but instead

you pick this old woman
who's not adept at playing ball.
And it's Saturday night so

the boys are out prowling around,
a favorite pastime, but here
you are, nudged beside me,

nodding off to a TV movie
we've both ignored before.
And I know, in the night you'll leave

your perfect bed, come spoon
the warmth of your sunshine fur
against my lonely curve, gaze at me

in the dark, moonlight glowing
from those slant gold eyes
envied by Egyptian kings.

Little cat, little cat,
how could I less than love you,
when you always choose me?

2nd Place, Grace Diane Jessen, Glenwood UT

Cats Rule

It has been said that cats have staff.
Before this thought provokes a laugh,
just think about that feline air
when cat reclines in your best chair.

Recall the times you offered food.
Your cat, disdainful, almost rude,
sniffed once or twice, then walked away
as there you stood in plain dismay.

Cats do display a queenly charm
and seldom act to cause alarm
so long as they can have their way
and you are careful to obey.

If it is true that cats are boss,
you may as well accept the loss
of role of master, but enjoy
the playful hours in their employ.

3rd Place, LaVern Spencer McCarthy, Blair OK

Taste-Test

"You will not eat a bean," I told my cat,
as she drew near and sang her begging song.
She eyed my bowl of pintos where they sat,
attempted to convince me I was wrong.
I sacrificed a tempting bit that she
might have a tasty bite of something light.
She circled like a vulture on a spree
for varmints that had perished in the night.
She sniffed the food a while, and I could tell
she thought its fragrant being fine and fair.
What feline could resist that bacon smell
that kissed the bean and lingered on the air?

But being such a picky carnivore,
she mangled it and left it on the floor.

1st Place, Randy K. Schwartz, Ann Arbor MI

Eclipse of the Pagan Spirits

Above a meadow in Norway
the sun was consumed by clouds.

Against the wind
the rushes bent with longing,
and the griffin-heads on the church
curled up like fiddles.

All in a great shadow
the spirits slid from the shingles,
and danced single file
into the forest.

2nd Place, Dennis Herschbach, Sartell MN

Driving at Night in Disappearing Farm Country

Out here, you can see forever.
Lights of prairie towns fill the night
like constellations dropped from heaven.
In the distance, solitary pinpricks shine
like distant stars dotting the horizon
where yard-lights mark farmsteads,
sites of struggles waged to survive
in a solitude bent on breaking the spirit.

Dusty, washboard roads follow
sections, half-sections, quarter-sections
in the form of square and rectangular plots.
Here and there in the dark
a farmer follows his tractor's beam
tracing invisible straight lines
as he works his land after sundown.

I roll down my car window,
let in the buzz of June bugs,
the rasp of crickets, the whisper
of breezes rattling com stalks,
sounds of a sleeping prairie.

I smell the fragrance of hay
mowed two days ago,
now ready to be windrowed
and baled, stored in a loft.
The aroma of the prairie
overwhelms my senses,

and across the nothingness,
farmstead lights are extinguished,
one by one.

3rd Place, Julie Martin, St. Paul MN

Jeffers Petroglyphs
—Comfrey, Minnesota

Stones have a spiritual essence which must be reverenced as a
manifestation of the all-pervading mysterious power that fills
the universe.   –Francis Lafleche, Omaha

An outcrop of Red Sioux Quartzite stretches for miles,
red to white, lavender-brown, lilac, red-purple.

The metamorphosed sandstone ranges and towers over
buffalo grass, little blue stem, and prickly pear cactus.

Ripples on the surface from an ancient Proterozoic sea,
multidirectional striations from glaciers, scratches, grooves.

Evening rakes low angles of light, petroglyphs appear—
images of turtle, buffalo, thunderbirds, people.

Near the glyph known as "First Woman,"
well-worn sandals rest outside the rope barrier.

Barefoot, the visitor kneels, reaches through time
to place fingertips on the hand emerging from rock.

Golden shadows play as light passes through
eastern amberwing dragonflies who shimmer

atop spikes of blue-violet prairie bush clover
swaying in hot, dry wind.

1st Place, Nancy Breen, Loveland OH

A March Night in Mariupol

Her frightened son clings to his orange bear
and inches closer to her on the bed
as warning sirens pierce the winter air.

She murmurs comfort, gently strokes his hair,
decides it might be safer if they fled.
Her frightened son clings to his orange bear,

unwilling to release it to her care.
She fills their bag with extra clothes instead
as warning sirens pierce the winter air.

She leads him to the basement stair by stair.
The lights go out. She tries her phone. It's dead.
Her frightened son clings to his orange bear

and worries that his father isn't there.
They flinch as something crashes overhead.
New warning sirens pierce the winter air.

Her husband is off fighting God-knows-where.
Each distant bomb blast fills her heart with dread.
Her frightened son clings to his orange bear
as warning sirens pierce the winter air.

2nd Place, Alison Chisholm, Birkdale Southport England

Blink of an Eye

I can't believe how fast the years have fled.
I hold my breath to try to hold back time.
There's far more life behind me than ahead.

Too busy living, no time to be dead,
it's hard, accepting that I'm past my prime.
I can't believe how fast the years have fled.

I'd relish freedom, travel, but instead
I work to earn a crust. This pantomime—
with far more life behind me than ahead—

acts out each scene at double speed. In bed
I lie awake and calculate. Crunchtime.
I can't believe how fast the years have fled.

A blur of marriage, children flown, I've shed
some duties, but lament (my constant whine)
there's far more life behind me than ahead.

A pile of tasks not done and books unread
reminds procrastination is a crime.
I can't believe how fast the years have fled.
There's far more life behind me than ahead.

3rd Place, Budd Powell Mahan, Dallas TX

Entropy

The Yellowstone caldera rumbles low,
as magma veils its threat in steaming air,
devolves toward a catastrophic blow.

Seismologists observe the signs and know
a blast could come, they urge us to prepare.
The Yellowstone caldera rumbles low,

the liquid rock emits an orange glow,
and mantle rises in its shift and tear,
devolves toward a catastrophic blow.

As mountains chafe and lava stirs to flow
and nature moves in waves of disrepair,
the Yellowstone caldera rumbles low.

A grassy slope sustains a fawn and doe,
but slides beneath a weight it cannot bear,
devolves toward a catastrophic blow.

A geothermal vent steams its tableau,
tectonic plates define the earthscape where
the Yellowstone caldera rumbles low,
devolves toward a catastrophic blow.

1st Place, Candy Lish Fowler, St. George UT

Each Night

he braids her hair

tresses cascade
like falling water

moonlight captures the nuance of curls

he runs his fingers through loose strands
and she
a quiet swan on a clear lake
bows her head

dark eyes flutter
warm skin glistens

breathing quickens as he
strokes long shafts of silk
and braids them
into folded wings

2nd Place, Terry Miller, Richmond TX

ritual of want

I crave ritual more than the gods
a dogma to tether my faith to the substantive
like soap in the eye its burn tells me
I am alive in two beings

ritual—two droppers of stevia
in my coffee   turn the dinner plate
twice before eating   feel the undercurrent

the periodic table of existence
ritual replaces a missing tenderness
with hard consonants and directionless diphthongs
no ooo's or ah's just a grocery list
of what's needed to sustain the body

while within   an impatient being
is in constant search for meaning

Fry Bread

Smoke curls from the hogan, and ponies paw dirt
searching for roots of white-top to ease the burn
between gaunt ribs. Inside, Nina pours water
into a wooden bowl of flour and salt, her practiced
hands melding the dough she will stretch and shape
then float in the cast iron skillet her mother gave her.

Family trusts the sizzling sound. Fragrant bread
must be enough with drifting snow closing roads,
and disease at every door ravaging the Rez
like a hungry wolf. This death, the old ones say,
reminds of long-ago days when white men
stole land and lives with sickness and lies.

Rosy dawn on sandstone and the squawk of crows
greet her as she gathers firewood with grandchildren.
Nina wails the chants of her people, a *Hozho* prayer
for a sanction from sky, for harmony with earth.
Fire smolders in the kitchen as she blends her dough,
and whispers a blessing on the flour and salt of another day.

1st Place, Diane Neff, Oviedo FL

Write Slowly, Dream Large

Write from your heart when the sad music calls,
Slowly the world will return to the light.
Dream gently, dream fiercely, with peace amid squalls,
Large is the story you're destined to write.

Slowly the world will return to the light.
Subtly we grow from each inch, every crawl.
Look to the trees, to the clouds, and the flight
Of the myriad wonders beyond self-made walls.

Dream gently, dream fiercely, with peace amid squalls
To lead you to nurture your strength, so you might
Explore with great care all your ramblings and scrawls
So their power can build as you reach your true height.

Large is the story you're destined to write,
Your narrative dance is both clipped and may drawl,
Your voice takes a lifetime to master, it's quite
A slow movement, but at the end, it's your all.
Write slowly, dream large.

2nd Place, Lori Anne Goetz, Germantown TN

Cold Winter Winds Swirling

Cold air swirls around our feet;
winter sweeps through every crack.
Winds attack both house and street,
swirling across the snowy track.

Winter sweeps through every crack.
The frosty room is homey and neat:
coats on their hooks, and a threadbare pack;
a whiff of tobacco, smoky and sweet.

Winds attack both house and street—
rattle the door to the tiny shack.
Icy boughs stoop in defeat
in gales like we knew on Kodiak.

Swirling across the snowy track,
a mixture of snow and sleet.
We sit inside, fire at our back,
stew on the stove, our daydreams sweet,

cold winter winds swirling.

3rd Place, Charles K. Firmage, Eloy AZ

She Was Always Riveting

She worked in a factory,
was happy to get hired,
always for victory,
riveting and fixing tires.

Was happy to get hired
as the men marched off to war,
nights she came home dog-tired,
awake, I could hear her snore.

Always for victory,
her rivets built the planes,
prayed the world would soon be free:
the blood, the sweat, the pain.

Riveting and fixing tires
till the boys come marching home,
reading letters by the fire,
wond'ring when Pop's coming home.
She was always riveting.

1st Place, Michael Spears, Plain City UT

Elsa's Dreams

The forest of Meuse-Argonne, France contains
14,246 tombstones of American soldiers killed in
action during that Offensive in World War One.

The gravel road running between the slanted
barn and chicken coop holds secrets lost
from ancient dust of summers long forgotten.
Wires, bent down and brown from too much sun
splash against burnt edges of the buildings.
Floorboards ache as wooden rockers creak,
like bare tree limbs in late October wind.
Elsa Jepsen rocks with the slow steady pitch
of wood on wood on the warping porch.
No dance of flame behind the rusted screen,
no flickering lick of lantern light,
just the horizon's slivered line of scarlet
drowning into obscurity.
The cold mantle above the fireplace
holds two identical pairs of baby shoes
covered with decades of dust.
Five thousand miles east two identical pairs
of army boots lie buried beneath
symmetrical crosses at Meuse-Argonne.
Elsa gazes at a faded photo of
the Oneida Academy basketball team,
eleven December, nineteen-fifteen.
Memories eclipse the borders of her brain,
as she struggles to recall which face
belongs with which twin's name.
There was a time when Elsa
dreamed of things beyond her fingertips:

grandchildren, birthday parties, sleep-overs,
Christmases filled with cheerful laughter.
Elsa Jepsen sips cold coffee from a stained
ceramic cup, uncleaned for eighty-seven days.
Wind whips dry leaves onto the porch
as she pulls her gray scarf snug around her neck
and continues rocking alone into the quiet night;
rocking, rocking, into the unknown dawn.

Last Bell

The Montmartre church
sounded its bells.
Celebrating something—
a wedding, end of a service,
or maybe just a winter sunset.

For my lover and me,
it was the end.
We had parted ways
on the streets
of Place de Clichy,
never to return.
At least not together.

I let him blame me.
He hit me again,
only the second time,
and shoved me,
saying it was ok now
because I'm just another guy.
I guess to show me
there's no going back.

Gathering his things,
long after the bells tolled,
he was angry,
I was sad.
I knew my tears
would have gotten to him
if he had seen them.
Nothing left to do
but tie up
a few loose ends.

We left no loose ends.

3rd Place, Jon Sebba, Murray UT

My Sister Sharbat

Early morning after dawn prayers I walk to madrassa.
They call me Little Pupil.
My sister leads Father's sheep and goats to grass.
They call her Little Goat.

I learn to read the Koran. We write with pencils.
Now my name is Little Scribe.
Sharbat watches the animals to keep the wolves away.
Her name is Little Goatherd.

We boys chant suras till we can sing them by heart.
They call me Little Scholar.
Sharbat can't read, she doesn't need to. Why should she?
They call her Little Tulip.

In madrassa I learn to count, to add and about money.
They call me Little Man.
Sharbat also learns to count to know if sheep are missing.
They call her Little Sharbat.

I can write my name in Dari and Pashto. One day my father
will tell me who I will marry. I will become a father of my family,
raise flocks of sheep and goats, own many wives.
I will be rich and they will call me Father.

A cameraman from a picture magazine came to Afghanistan.
He took a photograph of Sharbat unveiled.
She will marry rich, old Mr. Gula.
Father will get a big dowry when Sharbat is married
because she has green eyes and she is pretty.
She will cook food for the man, and be Sharbat Gula,
but most will call her Mr. Gula's Wife Number Four.

1st Place, Barbara J. Funke, St. George UT

Bonsai Poem

Bonsai: art of growing dwarfed ornamental trees
and shrubs in pots

A small bowl crowned with soil
accepts a seedling idea that slowly roots,
enjoys the mister's vapor, warming sun.
Possibilities ofphrase bud green:
young jungle-push through yielding air.

The poet plans to tame this rangy bush
crowded with crossed thoughts,
snapped and twisted leaves.
She studies first, then pries its slender limbs,
inserts discretion's blades, and nips.

> If a branching concept persists,
> establishing its girth and offshoots,
> an amputation by design is key
> to succoring the better of the two,
> fostering its character. And then

exacting pliers grip a line to bend. Taut wires
and bindings sleeve its tender bark
as poet guides to nuance every jointed phrase
and manages the branching twigs of words,
the polished gleam of emerald syllables.

Mature root crowns are bared,
old punctuation's gnarls distinctly carved.
When fresh moss is applied to mulch the ground,
the bonsai poem, now trained to lean
as if in furious wind one hundred years,

seems wiser still to show
how crafted beauty speaks.

2nd Place, Susan Chambers, Mankato MN

What I Want at My Funeral

There are three deaths. The first is when the body ceases to function.
The second is when the body is consigned to the grave. The third is
that moment, sometime in the future, when your name is spoken for
the last time.
      –David M. Eagleman, *Sum: Forty Tales from the Afterlives*

A sweet, single malt scotch for everyone
to toast each well-wisher about
every five minutes throughout the evening.
Raise your glass to good poems,
special music, everything that makes us laugh.

Read poems: my favorites from Ted Kooser, May Sarton,
William Stafford, Jane Hirschfield, Lee Young Li—
how can I name them all? There are so many!
And from all those retreats—we must read yours.

I want splashes of color; it could be flowers
in huge purple vases. Maybe a cornucopia of artwork.
Don't wear black—you in a red shirt, she in a blue dress.
Light up the whole room like a blazing rainbow.

Raise your voices: croon Broadway musical numbers
from *Wicked, Stop the World, The Secret Garden.*
Make sure you sing along. I want sweet Celtic numbers
with lots of harp. Belt out some Blood, Sweat and Tears.
Use *Adagio for Strings, Opus 11* by Barber as a grand finale.

It will be final, I guess. I know I won't be there
to see what you actually do. I have to trust
that you will make it a great party.

To those in charge: please don't be cheap.
Feed everyone a rousing first-rate dinner

with an excellent chocolate dessert.
Let them salute me one time at the end of the evening
with the finest of libations. No speeches,
but make sure people know I tried my best.

When everything is done, take home
some of my poems to read once more,
keep me from that third death.

3rd Place, Gwen Gunn, Guilford CT

Poets Will Survive

Siri schedules our appointments
robots make our cars
Deep Blue wins at chess

algorithms decide
who will be hired
paroled   or fired

computers grow proficient
at translation   stock picks
diagnoses of our ills

the Socially Aware Robot Assistant
senses the mood of her client—
OK but she can't walk like us   we gloat

yet we know touch and mobility
will be improved by us
the very ones put out of work

until they learn to fix themselves
robots will need to be
repaired   rescripted   redesigned

and though algorithms try bot art
paint pictures   write scenes   make music
programmers of poetry concluded:

*...even when you activate two discriminate networks that train a
recurrent neural network and link them to a deep-coupled visual-poetic
embedding model consisting of a skip-thought model, a part of speech
parser, and convolutional neural network—writing poems is hard.**

writing poems is human

*"How Frightened Should We Be of A.I.?" by Tad Friend, *The New Yorker*,
May 14, 2018

1st Place, Laurie Kolp, Beaumont TX

After the Funeral

I am driving through Iowa with the windows down. Turbines line the endless highway and stretch across fallow cornfields. As brisk wind moves through them, quiet hums become thunderous jets. It happens so fast, I get lost in the horizon, my gasping breath the sudden gusts, my raw emotions entangled DNA. No longer spiraling out of control, the rotors settle down again. They are symmetrical, perfectly dispersed, these rotating vanes cycling the air. Cogwheels through my mind. Rumbling thunder as I make my way to my childhood home. Interrupting all thoughts of what lies ahead handling Dad's estate.

whirlwind—
a bright red-tailed kite
sails skyward

Primera Comunión

Outside Holy Comforter Church the children are in two parallel lines; the boys with their slicked-back hair fidget in their shined black shoes—some borrowed and perhaps a bit too short or long, but they will not have to be worn all day. The girls, mini-brides, are under instructions to keep their white shoes unscuffed. Their dresses and veils too, unless saved from an older sibling or *prima,* might have come from the church's clothing exchange, the deep bin in the community room where volunteers sort and fold, where exactly what you're looking for, even a communion veil, can occasionally be fished up from the very bottom. The Miami morning is already hot; traffic streams by on 13th Avenue. Vigilant *mamis* adjust errant bows and monitor everyone's *comportamiento. Papis* mop sweat from their brows; it will be cooler inside the church.

> strains of organ music
> a shiver out of nowhere
> despite the pavement's heat

Primera comunión, un paso importantísimo in the *desarrollo* of the children's Christian lives—so says the bulletin the ushers are handing us. Afterwards there will be an *almuerzo* of *lechón asado, yuca, pasteles,* sugary punch to wash it all down, and *cafecitos* served in tiny paper cups, which the grownups will load up with cube upon cube of yet more sugar. Also, soft ripe mango slices sprinkled with lemon juice.

> smell of salty meat
> itchy petticoats
> await greasy fingers

Near the altar the conga-drum player is setting up. The incoming procession will strive for solemnity, but he will less loose for the *Gloria,* the *Sanctus* and the final hymn when the children process out in a blitz of *fotos.*

> white veils—foaming surf
> bodies borne by raft
> from open water

3rd Place, Russell Strauss, Memphis TN

Musings of a Picture Bride (1941)

I never wed in a shrine wearing *wataboshi,* or *shiromuku* to proclaim purity. Through a *nakodo*, my family received Haru's mailed picture, sent him mine. I alone signed documents for a simple civil wedding. My father, a street sweeper in Osaka, saw no other chance for my prosperity. *Haru* means springtime. I left as cherries bloomed.

> Pink fallen blossoms,
> shed after a single week.
> My dreams weep their loss.

Haru's photograph deceived me. He was fifteen years older than I, did not own the house and car before which he had posed. My Japanese wedding documents were unacceptable to Americans. On the dock, we were married again. Together we worked in the cane fields, our marriage brightened only by children who sprung wild like *Pua Aloalo*.

> Whispering offspring,
> like sun-faced hibiscus blooms,
> confide their secrets.

Like me, the honeybee was imported to these islands. This morning, bellicose bees bearing *Nippon*'s rising sun buzzed above the hive called Diamond Head. My dreams of return burst as bombs shattered the harbor. Even in moments of greater hope, I suspected, after so many years, I would never revisit the cherry blossoms of my youth.

> *Nene*, my omen,
> never flies from Hawaii.
> He seeks honor here.

Poet's note: Translations for words in the poem: "wataboshi" is a white wedding head-dress, "shiromuku" a wedding kimono, "nakodo" a marriage broker, and "Pua Aloalo" a Hawaiian yellow hibiscus. "Nippon" is Japan and "Nene" a native Hawaiian goose.

1st Place, Joyce Gregor, Westcliffe CO

The Sanctity of Snow

While viewing white lace cascading,
glazed branches
like harp strings,
play a Wedding March
and shadow maidens dance
on marble floors.

The Willow dressed in brocade cotton
bows like a country bride
in a winter garden.
Embroidered snow patterns
of bird feet prints
stitch designs on her gown,
and hoarfrost adds rhinestone
buttons to adorn the bodice.

The Willow dressed in brocade cotton
bows like a country bride
in a winter garden.
Angel hair girdles her crown,
her countenance, an opal radiance
as the virgin awaits her lover
to melt the icy buttons
opening her to spring.

While viewing white lace cascading,
I wait—wait for my lover
to strum an Appalachian Spring in me,
rejuvenating my winter season
into a spirit dancing
on a marble floor.

2nd Place, George Wylie, Wyandotte MI

The Soaring of Mornings

It was almost silent
The land below the eagle was misty
and the land rose towards him
as the sun created dimension and movement
A train muttered and wormed its way along a hillside
Its whistle muted as if paying respect to the morning
The trees grew shadows and color as they gained strength
wondering if they had the valor to pierce another day
Agreeable mists had floated over the ponds and streams
And now they succumbed to the stronger boldness of breezes
Some sheep earned their way up a rise with new lambs wobbling by
And the sun stole back the moisture it had given to the night
The noises climbed slowly to the soaring bird and he knew them well
A creature of focus, his attention ignored the routines to find his prey
He knew where to fly his shadow to benefit his pursuit
He knew he was the supreme undaunted presence of this morning
A tractor dusted its way down a tree-lined road, scattering some swallows
A green heron worked the shallows of a glimmering pond
creating small noiseless ripples in nature's mirrors
And two mallards veed the surface on their way to some place or another
Daytime curls up a land that darkness flattens
It pulls the hills towards the sky and cups the land into valleys
And it lets out to play the young rabbits for the eagle to see
And he gracefully accepts their contribution to another day on his land
Nature at its best is repetition and replacement
It has to offer succor to keep the mornings coming, the eagles flying
It must slumber and it must eat. Else it becomes far too silent.
And all that is left is an abandoned train, rusting its way into a hill.

3rd Place, Barbara Blanks, Garland TX

At Spring Creek Forest Preserve on Her Birthday

It is a dreamy place, shadowed, like stepping back
through time into primitive beauty. A trail meanders
through the preserve, trees and undergrowth
on one side, canyon's abyss on the other.

A shallow, sun-warmed ocean covered
much of this area 87 million years ago.
Gradually, it receded, leaving layers of silt,
mud, and the bodies of minuscule creatures.
Over millennia, Spring Creek gnawed
through the remains, creating canyon walls
flush with Cretaceous fossils, and compressed
into flakey, white Austin Chalk limestone.

Only here do Chinquapin, bur and Shumard oaks
grow together—some are 300 years old,
rare remnants of a virgin forest.
Roughleaf dogwoods and elderberry shrubs,
lush with creamy white flowers,
nestle into the understory alongside
corralberrys, with their wispy teardrop leaves.
The beautyberry's fountain of arching
branchlets are weighted with purple clusters.
Golden groundsel carpets the ground
with tiny yellow flowers. Tucked in here and there—
the nodding blankets of Solomon's seal
and trout lily's ephemeral yellow blooms.

No city noise. Just bird calls, the whirring
of insects, and a slight breeze rustling dried leaves.
At a break in the foliage, I step off the path,
approach a ledge overlooking the water.
My mother called herself a "rare fossil."
I'm sure she will feel perfectly at home here,
ashes scattered amongst her "contemporaries."

1st Place, Candy Lish Fowler, St. George UT

Act III

Nature's hourglass holds the season.
Crimson blush on gilded pear,
Fall's bounty bends branches of time.

Plump peaches and prime apples spice the air.
Sun is lazy-late in a sky of slanted blue
and I feel a change.

Leaves begin.

Supple vibrant life *wilts and falls.*
In a storm of amber, orange and red,
their downpour covers the ground.

Written on each withered leaf is a collection,
a colorful memoir; clouded loss, moonlit doubt,
and a season of joy.

Without warning, a faint brittle sound.
Parchment layers swept by wind,
swirl into funnels. Some spin away.

Who will gather the memories?

The tallest tree stands empty.
Stark skeletal branches hold no stories.
But, I am here…and I will remember
      the hope
      in a crocus pushing up through the last thin crust of snow—

      the promise
      in seeing a new foal stand for the first time—

      the joy
      bursting in a brilliant summer morning—

      the love
      held in November's final roses.

2nd Place, Nancy Simmonds, Fort Wayne IN

Ghostflowers

An ekphrastic poem inspired by a wood
block print of Katsushika Hokusai, poem
by Bunya no Asayasu, ca. 1835-36

When autumn breezes
begin to bend the dying reeds
the girls, the beautiful girls
go out into their boats
go out onto the lake
harvest waterlilies
cover their flat-bottomed boat
with a carpet of green and of white.

Ghostflower tea
shapeshifts our winter
into memories of autumn days

when the girls
the beautiful girls
go out into their boats
go out onto the lake
when waterlilies
cover their flat-bottomed boat
bruised under their tiny feet.

3rd Place, Jenna Pashley, Richmond TX

The Poet Is Antimony

The poet is antimony,
all jagged
around the edges,
raw, untreated, charged.

She is ready
to blacken the eyes
of anyone who presses her
the wrong way.

Luster hides friction,
she resists the fists,
closes her own around
a pencil, darkens her own
eyes with kohl, marks
elemental pages
with silvered incantations,

all jagged around the edges,
she is antimony,
strikes her match head
and flares.

1st Place, Crystie Cook, Sandy UT

Quiet Meanderings of Chopin

Ah, Chopin, your ornamentation adds
another layer of liquid grace,
where the languid, fluid left hand in broken chords
has prevailed with a rhythm of souls, voices,
gentle victories in the world of sound.
Sonorous thoughts, tiny grace notes
fall like smallbuds,
content to be shaken off and arranged,
in a pattern as pretty as an infant breathing.

All the quietness of spring, summer, fall, and winter
merge and meld in a meandering journey.
Seventy-seven measures must mean love—
lucky once, lucky twice.
And in fact, this gentle love gives the music
permission to stroke the happier side of melancholy,
to explore a bit of B flat minor, where
the left hand has a stable, cushioning beauty
and sense of its own melodic worth.

It is true, of course, that even the most perfect love
is full of complementary ideas, imagined caresses,
and a piano full of technique both simple and advanced,
like streams and creeks running into green,
shining like golden, blue, and white-light blossoms,
where grass, reeds, and willow branches drift
in a slow, low river,
toward life,
toward memory,
toward eternity of meaning.

Note: This poem treats Chopin's *Nocturne, Op. 27, No. 2 in
D-Flat Major,* Lento sostenuto.

2nd Place, LaVern Spencer McCarthy, Blair OK

Garden Sale

I sold a dozen villanelles today.
Each one was beautiful, unique and whole.
My sonnets went for more than most could pay.
I grew them in the garden of my soul.

Each one was beautiful, unique and whole.
My wild haikus were taken, row by row.
I grew them in the garden of my soul,
a special place that only I would know.

My wild haikus were taken, row by row
I planted them anew for later on.
A special place that only I would know
will care for them until their words have grown.

I planted them anew for later on.
The sunlight will caress them for a while—
will care for them until their words have grown.
My poetry abounds with grace and style.

The sunlight will caress them for awhile.
I wrote them with the colors of the sky.
My poetry abounds with grace and style
with bright quatrains for sale to all who buy.

I wrote them with the colors of the sky.
My efforts made them somehow more divine.
With bright quatrains for sale to all who buy,
I polished them with joy and made them shine.

I wrote them with the colors of the sky.
My sonnets went for more than most could pay.
With bright quatrains for sale to all who buy.
I sold a dozen villanelles today.

3rd Place, Diane Neff, Oviedo FL

A Sonnet for the Old House

The house, defying gravity and wind,
stood upright, although covered in debris,
the branches fallen from the leafless tree
on stained and rusted roof, now tangled, pinned
to bared and bleached wood sides, like rough scraped skin.
An early winter scene, a memory
of joyous times, a gathering of we,
a family sharing love, and still we grin.
Our pride at weathering the brutal storm
of deaths, of losses great and small we bore,
but holding tight to hope within the strife,
ignoring broken windows, we stay warm
through strength of history. Our family's core
will hold this home intact, throughout this life.

1st Place, Connie Green, Lenoir City TN

Aubade in Late October

What squint of eye can reveal the fog
rising above the river as more than

mirage, can transport this moment into centuries
past when only the brown thrasher scratched

these fallen leaves, when only the eagle flew
over the river, and morning came unmarked,

undated, one more turn in the seasons' slow dance,
a speck caught up in the avalanche of the years?

What sight line angling into the pasture
where turkeys bob their heads in time

with hunger that sends their beaks down,
down, down into fallen seed of millet, milo,

wild grasses left by the spendthrift summer,
what wild vision places them back before

we humans trod these hills, perhaps into eras
before stardust and good luck mingled to form

the first upright forefather who would stand
atop this peak and stare in astonishment?

2nd Place, Cheryl Van Beek, Wesley Chapel FL

Seeing Inside Out

*A painter should paint not only what he has in front of him, but
also what he sees inside himself….Close your bodily eye, that you
may see your picture first with the eye of the spirit. Then bring to
light what you have seen in the darkness, that its effect may work
back, from without to within. If he sees nothing within, then he
should stop painting what is in front of him.*

–Caspar David Friedrich

A branch tapping at your window,
a line of verse,
Venus sharing a nightcap with the moon,
whatever blooms at you out there—
don't copy it, or explain it,
or try to understand it from outside.

Take a cutting. Let its stem pierce
the fertile soil of your breath.
Stake it in the place where fledglings start,
where it's moist and vermiculite loose.
Its node buried in the dark peat of your roots,
teach it to find its way, stretch toward the light inside you.

Feed it thoughts and tears.
Let your memories and microbes
prism it ultraviolet.
Visit the earth within you
the water, the dark, the light, the waves.

Seed-split jolt, crack of loam in your soul,
smell the green sprout into a garden.
Watch it leaf out in your song,
page, canvas, the hands of others.

3rd Place, Budd Powell Mahan, Dallas TX

Two Visions of a Garden
for the Neighbor Called to Nurse a Dying Son
a rondeau redouble

I walk the stone-laid path where iris grow,
the rhizomes' crowding fills abandoned soil,
and visions animate you in the slow
decisive rhythm of a blissful toil.

As absence leaves the weedy vines to coil,
the garden bakes in arid status quo.
As undercurrents spawn from summer boil,
I walk the stone-laid path where iris grow.

Too far away to see, you cannot know
the infiltration skews the quatrefoil
of beds' design and seismic dirt cracks show
the rhizomes' crowding fills abandoned soil.

A year has passed since duty came to spoil
the daily nurture of a hoe's soft blow,
but now the vision blurs as seen through oil
and visions animate you in the slow

intrigue of earth that seemed to stir and sow
a deeper harvest than a tool could roil.
I miss the garden played fortissimo,
decisive rhythm of a blissful toil

that weaved a spell from morning's dewy noil.
Until familiar step returns the glow
to plots grown over, clods of thrusting soil,
trust sustenance from every sky and know
I walk the stone-laid path.

1st Place, Julie Kim Shavin, Fountain CO

Snake

When I was a teen
we saw a snake in the basement.
Our parents stopped speaking to one another
around this time.
They passed in the hall, silent,
moved aside, silent.

Three months after our father died,
our mother announced,
we're starting a new chapter now!—
as though we were fiction,
a hoped-for bestseller,
as though we were pages that hated
their working title.
Something in me went slack.

For a long time
we were afraid of the snake.
Our mother had made our father
move his office down there.
He had quit his Tiparillos and
I didn't know how he managed,
though I was unacquainted with nicotine,
except second-hand.

Loneliness wrapped me like new skin.
It was cold and dank.
The ping-pong table
splayed its chronic quietude.
Its little net was always broken.
Everyone was a winner.

We read ourselves into a future
in which the snake became just a footnote.
Like our father.

2nd Place, Christine Irving, Denton TX

The Open Book

He says, he reads me like a book,
but his shelves lean heavily toward memoir,
biography and photo albums full of snapshots
photoshopped with nostalgia and sentiment.

I know how to make him laugh, to comfort,
to curb my tongue. He's never learned to read
between the lines, rarely glimpses the full
range of characters, who dwell behind
my pleasant face and dancing eyes.

0 yes, we dance in here. We wail and vibrate—
pungent, syrupy, and transparent. My shelves
retain a smattering of mystery, fantasy and sci fi,
volumes on Jung, quantum physics, symbol and myth.

I confess to a secret sweet tooth for romances,
but only those depicting a feisty heroine who claims
sovereignty before succumbing on her own terms.
My life is not a secret—everything displayed openly,
spines faced forward. But I loathe self-help books.

Never owned a manual. Guess he's on his own.

3rd Place, Patricia Barnes, Wyandotte MI

One Must Belong to a Book Club

We are the Blizzard/Tornado/Flood Book Club.
Our gatherings are scheduled for when it's impossible to meet.

We don't like each other, only the books.
Neither do we care for each other's opinions, only the books.

If a stranger asks, "Why are you reading *that*?"
We blame it on the book club, and read on.

We carry our books in brown wrappers for recognition.
We nod but don't speak.

Last year there was an unexpected break in a winter storm.
We were required to meet.

The hostess served saltines and soda.
We talked fast and left early.

Our annual newsletter is a list of twelve books
and potential meeting dates

to be canceled by weather reports.

1st Place, Patricia Tiffany Morris, Bondurant IA

somehow–somewhere

somehow
              somewhere
hiding in the dark
              shining in the light
dreading
              longing
to let go of
              to embrace
our child
              our only child

we were lost
              and found
in the confusion between stories
              in the moments before dawn
she breathed through pain
              she took our breath away

it was her death
              her life
that caused
              that showed
our hearts to pray
              our hearts to love

our child
              our baby
too soon
              too long
taken
              waiting
for heaven
              for heaven's gift

but home
              she's home
and I'm still here
              today somehow
loving through tears
              and living with hope

2nd Place, Diane Glancy, Gainesville TX

Ruth and Myrtle Wood

My grandmother's first child did not survive birth.
My grandmother said it nearly killed her too.
        Ruth Adelaide Wood
         August 13, 1908
          Of Such Is the Kingdom of Heaven
Is that where Ruth went?
Did she become a cherub like the cherubs
        in Corrado Giaquinto's *Adoration*
        of the Holy Cross on the Day of the Last
        Judgment?
Or did she have a chance to live on another plane?—
        the p-brane physicists call an *imagined world*
        where she married and I have an uncle
        and cousins I don't know?
Or do babies dead on arrival fall into the unknown
        like Susan Rothenberg's *Endless,*
         in which a figure barefoot and outlined in black
         tumbles upside-down on a white canvas?
What recompense is there for such an early death?
What is possible for a traumatized mother
        when there are no answers?
Their separation at birth, one to death,
        the other slowly back to life, but marked
        with the death of her infant.
What was it like as she stood at the grave
        of her first born
        in that wind-blown country cemetery?
Was my grandmother thinking, *of such is the kingdom*?

3rd Place, Susan Chambers, Mankato MN

Sunday Expectations

Tomorrow is Monday. I will take up tasks,
wear lawyer clothes again, pretend to understand truth.
I will write the brief for Grandma to keep granddaughter
safe from violent intrusions. I will talk to the Judge
for Mother. Son feels like he is at Gettysburg.
I move into each week, butt against demands to be perfect.

Tuesday father's daughter is lost, taken by a drunken mother.
His nightmares keep him awake.
Thursday a pickup truck passes. I shiver,
imagine the angry spouse rising, gun in hand,
to fire at changes they cannot stop. This time
I make it to the car, no bullets, only wind, weary as I am.

Late Friday I cry "enough!" rise from my desk.
I turn off lights, ignore the phone.
I remember for the first time a promise
to call my son's teacher. Too late.
I close my eyes, see his tight face
as I tell him I forgot yet again.
In bed I collapse, my heart off beat,
I count in the erratic rhythm the tempo of
two dozen lives. In the dark I struggle
to remember the unity of two.
Saturday, I wake to sun. We rake the yard, clear off
old debris, sing as we walk the familiar trail to the river.
On this rainy Sunday afternoon I bake a perfect chicken
while my children laugh over Monopoly.

Tomorrow is Monday. I never fail to put my suit back on,
my body not quite recovered from knots of weekday wearing.
I lift up files; burden myself with their weather cycles.

On Monday morning I rise before the sun,
leave family still huddled in night.
I pace two miles with a dog who runs ahead of me—
like my clients' demands; like the needs of so many children.
The first rays pierce the newly harvested fields
while birds sing morning, as if Mondays had never been invented.

1st Place, James D. Neiswender, Denton TX

Minnow

I reach into a pile of family photos,
pull one out showing me as a small boy,
shorts, no shirt, a dress tie around my neck.
I am looking into the camera,
but I don't remember the exact moment
the shutter clicks open and shut in the black box.
Other photos freeze me in time,
rowing a boat, a large awkward paddle,
or my brother sitting beside me on the middle seat,
and Mom driving the wooden hull,
her hand on the throttle-handle
of the Evinrude motor,
her laughing smile.

I remember a fishing trip
with Dad driving the boat.
A slippery minnow flips from my hand
into the river beside the moving craft.
I grab for it, but miss, falling overboard.
As I go underwater, Dad catches my collar
and pulls me up and out of the water
in one motion back to safety.
I am not scared, only wet,
until I see the terror on Mom's face.
My eyes fill with tears at the danger I escaped.
Family, laughing in good-natured ribbing,
tells this story,
Jim swims with fish.

2nd Place, Meredith R. Cook, Blue Earth MN

Training

The house shakes until windows rattle.
Thundering noise drowns out the clock.
The kittens are playing racing battle
Until it is not safe to walk.

Swish, swish, swish to the other room
One, two, three zip past my feet,
Pounce on each other, chew, and zoom
Back past me fast on their retreat.

White, black, striped—single file—
Striped, black, white—they run through.
I don't block their racing-aisle.
They chew each other, chase, and chew.

As for what they think, that's plain:
They think they are a chew chew train.

3rd Place, Viktor Tichy, San Mateo IA

Genius Parrot

Pam had a parrot
with feathers like gold.
He talked more than Pam,
and knew more than he told.

She served him groats
in a bowl of pure gold.
He pecked at her nose
and said, "Pam has a cold."

She poured green tea
in her red china cup,
he perched on her head
and said: "Pam, hurrrry up."

She packed her lunch
to bring it to work;
he circled his cage,
and sang: "Forrrgot a forrrk."

"When in Walmarrrt, Pam,
get matching knife,
then stop in the pet shop
and buy me a wife."

1st Place, Lorrie Wolfe, Windsor CO

Black Shoes

after Kaveh Akbar

Black orthopedic shoes are tumbling from the closets. Black Flamenco shoes are striking the floorboards in staccato stutters. I throw a stick. The dog retrieves black shoes. His muddy paws are also black shoes. The garden pushes up enough black shoes to fill baskets and dinner plates. Dead tree limbs are black shoe-tongues stretching across the sky. Stars fall onto asphalt to light a path for explorers' black shoes. Teenagers with black nail polish take selfies with black shoes. Old men in black wingtips admire the ankles of women in black shoes. Mothers decorate their babies' wrists with black shoelaces holding balloons. Babies in bracelets learn to walk in black shoes. Thunderhead clouds rise like the heels of black shoes. Hail pounding the sidewalks becomes a symphony of black shoes. I am rooted to this earth by the ache in your black support shoes and comforted by the familiar sibilance of black shoes slippering across a polished floor. In memory's black hallway, your black shoes echo. Wide feet in old-fashioned black shoes anchor me against the darkest windy doubts of midnight. Oh, Grandma, in these troubled times, I need you with me now.

2nd Place, Emory D. Jones, Iuka MS

New Year II: A Golden Shovel Poem

...There was not much that was ahead of him,
And there was nothing in the town below—
Where strangers would have shut the many doors
That many friends had opened long ago.
  –Edwin Arlington Robinson, "Mr. Flood's Party"

When the new year is about to dawn out there
And the old year is dying, we think of what was
There, and we regret what we had not
Done in the past year and how much
We could then have done to help that
Person that we know. We wonder what was
The answer to our regrets then look ahead
To find out what we hoped could be of
Our resolutions we made with him,
Who is our friend, to keep him close and
We would like to know that we were there
When he needed us and knew that he was
Grateful for our help and that nothing
Would keep us from mutual support in
Whatever way that we could help the
Friend in this new year and in this town
When we can be thankful that we are below
The New Year's stars this night where
We receive with open arms strangers
That we have met and welcomed would
Become new friends and have
Good times at New Year's parties that shut
The Old Year out, and close the
Door on the old year. Many
Of the ones that we bring in our doors
That we invite along with some that

We have met anew but now greet as many
Old older ones that had been friends
And neighbors of ours that we had
Celebrated many New Years and opened
Each one with joy for the New Year as long
As we remember that we celebrated years ago.

3rd Place, Shari Crane Fox, Grass Valley CA

Ditching Therapy

I'm getting colonic hydrotherapy now, my patient tells me, so I won't be
back and you're too expensive anyway, and she is sitting in front of me with

hair newly bleached and spiked and a new smoky eye, and she looks great
aside from a short skirt that shines like a hummingbird because she is

spreading her legs to flash me beneath that skirt and asking what I'm doing
this Friday night, so I know she's secretly stopped her medication.

I've had patients leave me for vitamin infusions, herbal tinctures, and bad
boyfriends. I've had patients leave for the bottle, backsliding, backstabbing
or backing up because they didn't like their new set of eyes. But this?

Colon: rhythmical unit of utterance, used to draw attention to a matter,
referee between ratios, conductor to strophic stanzas, one dot balancing on
top of another to say stop, look at me, look what's coming. Yeah. About that ...

Today I am a poor colon, a semicolon at best, so she leaves therapy
early to go next-door to the new colonic hydrotherapy center advertised by

the sandwich board on the sidewalk outside my office, a sandwich board
I contemplated throwing into the shrubbery just this morning.

Now, I regret my restraint. There are times when you see one patient,
and even as you help the others, that one patient taps at your amygdala

like an in-law at the back door that knows you're home and not answering. At
the end of the workday, I'm ready to hear the click of my key in the door.

As I step out, I hear arguing, and see the colonic hydrotherapist waving
an unfiltered cigarette like a laser pointer in a lecture. She's screaming at her

phone about who should've ordered the gloves.
Okay, judge me—I couldn't help but take a look at her nails.

Before I Sleep

I take the measure of my day.
I tape how tall, how wide, how deep,
and gauge the harvest that I reap.
I tally prices, costs—too cheap?
too steep?—what portions should I weigh?

My time is full of work and play,
with shares of sunshine and of gray
experiences in a heap.
I take the measure.

As I take stock I have to say
my gratitude exceeds dismay.
The sum and substance makes me weep
with joy for all that's in my keep.
For more of such rich life I pray.
I take the measure.

2nd Place, Christine Irving, Denton TX

Absent

The heart's gone out of home without you here.
Our home becomes but house without you near.
Who would have thought a place could so transform
or loneliness this soon become the norm?
Your silent voice rings in my inner ear.

Old friends will find me lacking in good cheer
unwilling now to share a laugh or beer.
Nothing feels cold or hot, it's all lukewarm,
the heart's gone out of home.

Rich colors fade, like verdant leaves gone sere,
who would have thought that scarlet could look drear
or sadness paint each wall thus uniform?
I long for cyclone's cloud and summer's storm
to raze this space I once held very dear.
The heart's gone out of home.

3rd Place, Julie Kim Shavin, Fountain CO

In Pastures Gold

In pastures gold the heady deer
fly swift across the vast plains sere
while both, in sky, hang sun and moon
as though all life were late and soon—
the days and nights do same appear.

Into this nexus I appear
with mind disturbed and body queer
from sleep thrice hacked before the noon
in pastures gold.

I often feel things dread and drear,
like life's one chance, so quick, severe—
but Chinook winds, if winter-hewn,
today are sweet, a soothing tune
to all who, lucky, roam out here
in pastures gold.

1st Place, Laura Mahal, Fort Collins CO

a memorial to red: for a young man who found peace only in nature
(Trigger warning: subject of suicide)

I knew a boy who shot himself
yet first, he made a video,
which his mother showed at the memorial

The boy said: "Look for the reds,"
except he said, "f***ing" reds, and now, for me,
every autumn leaf, not green, not orange, not yellow, not brown,

is red,
and when I walk in the piney woods, a memorial,
I see red things: trash, a mule deer's tongue, flashes of color, stifling color

Now, red is death,
too young to die, this boy,
and my love for a color: raspberries, toenail polish, sunburnt noses…eviscerated

I look for the green,
the gold, the Ponyboy, football games, pigskin brown, shoulder pad foam,
colorful cleats,
I'm blinded by red

This boy he went
with him went the trash, mule deer munching, maple leaves, strawberries,
he left me no gold, pine green, or yellow

Blue is not effing blue
it is baby blue and boyhood,
a memorial to what might have been

Gold, not to be. Old, not for him.
No autumn orange. No fading out. He flamed from this world in shotgun fire,
he didn't expire, he died.

He took red with
and his mother's heart, broken,
yet beats…a memorial to red.

2nd Place, Budd Powell Mahan, Dallas TX

The Great Sioux War

The U.S. gave the Black Hills to the Sioux,
but broke that pledge in lust for new-found gold,
and pillaged what the native people knew
was theirs alone to claim from times of old.

With guile another white man's promise died.
another war against invader's greed,
as tribes united, would not be denied
the ownership of land they would not cede.

So Custer died in Little Bighorn rout
a failure of integrity and skill,
his bloody end a whimper not a shout,
a final stand on green Lakota hill.

We teach the battle, boast our history,
ignoring fact, creating travesty.

Household Chores

Soft moccasins
On sandy trail
Climb upward
Now to slope
Of stone,
Cliffside home,
Caves worn smooth
By generations
Of habitation,
Cook fires' smoke
Rises
Near racks of drying
Hides,
Strips of meat,
And sinew for
string,
And the small feet
Now stop,
Delivering water
To the waiting pot.

1st Place, Sandra McGarry, Fort Collins CO

I Do Not Know the Potter

I do not know the hands.
I do not know the glaze.
I do not know the kiln's heat.
Yet each morning, I choose the blue cup
swirled at the handle.
My wife of many coffee days asks,
"What happens if you don't have that cup?"
I look at her bewildered.

"Why wouldn't I?"

I bought the cup at a morning market
beneath an overpass in Jacksonville, Florida.
This before the preachers
let the houses of prayers empty out.
Before the sun reigned high in the sky.

This morning I slather butter onto raisin toast
watch it disappear.
Hold my cup with two hands like an offering
the way I've seen the clergy do.

Take this. And I do
eat my bread and drink from my cup.

2nd Place, Courtney Moody, Ellenton FL

Florida Anatomy

My hair is kudzu taking over highway love handles
and sprinkler-speckled backyards.
>> My eyes are theme park gates scratching over concrete
>>> to the human dawnflood.
>> My ears are sinkholes filling up with the sound of sand trembling
>>> like 65 degrees.
>> My nose is a fresh spring hiding caverns once woven beneath
>>> the pan and handle.

My teeth are an eternal battle between a gator, a green bull,
a knight, and a native warrior.
>> My lips are homes painted with pastels and stained
>>> with words from Hemingway.
>> My neck is an overflowing gutter dripping with the stormy bane
>>> of tourist dreams.
>> My chest is a bundle of orange blossoms drifting up and down
>>> the groves in April.

My arms are sabal palm branches hanging like descending angels
and waltzing in the wind.
>> My fingers are lizard tails as long as SR A1A and discarded
>>> at a hawk claw's touch.
>> My stomach is an airboat rumbling and churning the slush
>>> of Everglade swampland.
>> My hips are glass skyscrapers blended in sunsets before
>>> humidity coats panes in steam.

My thighs are manatees breaking the sparkle-surface for sunlight
to trickle over their backs.
>> My calves are dolphins rescued from failing fins and finding
>>> resurrection in silence.

My ankles are roadside orange stands rooted in the ground and old
     as Ponce de Leon.
My toes are sandgrains drifting off of vacation edges
     into the Atlantic and the Gulf.

My mind is a hurricane turning over itself as it searches for a home
that will stay warm forever.
     My saliva is ocean water filled with enough salt to flavor food
          until snowbirds migrate.
     My blood is red tide sneaking through sandgrain mazes
          and slipping into seashell cracks.
     My veins are trains carrying oranges to a claustrophobic doom
          and acrobats to destiny.

My tendons are the small towns with 3-digit populations and names
big as Zora Neale Hurston.
     My nervous system is I-4 on a 5 o'clock Friday with metal rainbows
          baking in the sun.
     My heartbeat is a sandhill call singing against a backdrop
          of Latin rhythm and concrete.
     My heart is a rocket rising from the home of cruises and genies
          and shooting for Mars.

3rd Place, Barbara J. Funke, St. George UT

Butterfly Effect
Butterfly Garden Miami

I've read a single wing-beat
a hemisphere away
might fan a distant war
from factions' discontent,
unsettling
the continents like dominoes.

A friend's well-crafted lines
blend butterflies and bicycle wheels,
to share her expectation's churn
toward birth. Connection:
why can't a single wing-beat
save the world?

Great circle flown from snow
to tropic haven,
I feel the glass-roofed sanctuary
close its chrysalis around me.
Untraceable confusion of delight,
tiny stained-glass wings
flirt with my hair and eyelashes.
Elegant nine-inch spans at rest
pose, palettes serene.

Recalling metamorphoses
and world migrations
in this cheeky breeze
of a billion-trillion flutters,
scores of wingless aliens
like you and me

explore the garden—
calm eye in the daily storm.
We slow with gentled step,
thrilled to peace
that gauzy flits of butterfly
lift heavy souls,
convert the hungry worm
to flight.

1st Place, Cade Huie, Grand Prairie TX

Foreshadowing You

Your ghost will come,
will descend through to me, yes—
the door will be left open a crack,
enough for you to wisp into,
your smoky silk a molten air entering,
bidden by my whispering blood.

Oh, I will sink into your lost flame,
remembering your moonlit steps
in the sand as you swayed
like light to the silent moon's singing,
like a water weed in the tide.

Yes—your ghost in my breath held long
to taste you, exhaled into my hand
to pool into warmth, spreading;
your ghost in my bleeding,
drowning out grief.

Oh, your voice the wine,
my ears the cup—
your touch the pen,
my skin the page—
yes, your eyes the sky,
my heart the bird—
your ghost my madness,
my promise,
my hymn.

2nd Place, Crystal Barker, North Las Vegas NV

Diamonds and Deodorant

The famous Beverly Hills Rodeo Drive,
(pronounced Ro-Day-O),
where salespersons
who could pass as GQ models
await customers' arrival
to unlock glass-covered cases
of Cartier diamonds:
princess, Asscher, emerald and radiant;
glistening rings, pennants,
even loose,
scattered as confettied decoration;
no price tag is placed in sight,
secured,
just in case there is a tempted lifter—
for such wanted things are so highly valued.
It's different there.
On my side of town,
Baldwin Hills Rodeo Road,
(pronounced Ro-D-O),
just renamed Obama Blvd.,
where salespersons,
tired and crumpled,
retrieve a key from behind the counter
to unlock glass-covered cases
of CVS deodorant and razors:
Degree, Old Spice, Axe
Gillette, Schick, Venus;
no decoration,
most price marked as $3.29,
secured,
just in case there is a tempted lifter—
for such needed things are so highly valued.
It's different here.

3rd Place, Vicki Arnett, Preston MO

Turtles

Tender-bodied creatures,
hidden in tough shells

Courageous hearts,
prepared to give

Ancient eyes,
that have seen it all

Strong claws,
to dig and build a nest

Did otter
pile mud on you

to break
Sky Woman's fall?

1st Place, V. Kimball Barney, Kaysville UT

Forever
(Shakespearean sonnet)

Forever is a long, long, time, my dear,
so don't make promises that you can't keep,
but love me just as long as you are here;
I want to feel your presence as I sleep.

I know you 're trying hard just to believe
that you can always stay right here with me,
but you're the only one you can deceive;
I know your inner yearning to be free.

It's quite all right; I'll get along just fine
when you are gone. There's nothing I can do
to change things, but at least for now you're mine.
I'll take as much as I can get of you.

Go on, take off and give free life a whirl;
I'll let you know if it's a boy or girl.

2nd Place, Barbara Blanks, Garland TX

Twelve Hours in the ER
(Shakespearean sonnet)

How easily she died: the fall on floor
of tile—the fractured skull and broken hip—
no harbinger that indicated more,
to hint at angels hovering, no tip
that warned of bleeding in her brain until
she wouldn't rouse—did not respond at all.
A "cat scan" told the story, clawed with chill
of dread. I never felt more helpless, small.
The stalking beast of grief was crouched nearby,
just barely held at bay. Meanwhile, I sat,
her hand in mine, and … waited … watched her die.
It doesn't get more intimate than that.
    She left me in the middle of the night.
    I shiver in the absence of her light.

The Cello and the Bow
(Shakespearean sonnet)

She yawns awake in sleepy breath, a sigh
when bow alights upon a single string
which starts a flood of notes. She marvels why
this simple touch would make her body sing.
Her neck feels fingers searching in caress
as bow begins its move across her waist.
The cellist's tune becomes a lover's guess
when harmony might change to anxious haste.
Melodic music finds delightful bliss
when boundless minutes lose their count of time,
until the tempo turns to urgent kiss
as cadence alters pageant's paradigm.
    The cello and the bow perform as one
    so long as music plays till both are done.

The Memory of Cells

After 14 days, every part of the epidermis
sloughed and flaked and drifted
its way to dust. They took with them
the memory of touch. It took 365
for the liver to screen and sift
and clean my blood of every trace.

It wasn't that you were toxic.
But the body remembers.

Hair, which has no nerve cells,
collects its data at the root.
It took six years to lose all that.
Bones, which seem so solid,
are a porous storehouse of minerals—
phosphorous, calcium, magnesium.
It took at least ten years
to replace that framework.

It wasn't that you were a foundation.
But the body remembers.

The cells in the eyes, forming
images in the mind, have died
and regrown. Even the hungry
sensors of sound and taste and smell—
that whole body is gone. Only
the firing neurons of the mind,
and their memories, remain.

It wasn't that you made many.
But I remember.

2nd Place, Lorrie Wolfe, Windsor CO

A Community of One

I am a woman
I am a woman writer parent
I am an unemployed woman writer mother grandmother
currently working on a book novel poem

I am a tea drinker middle aged experienced homeowner
former grant-writer realtor in recovery from
Reform Judaism escaped from suburbia
College graduate day dreamer
Nonsmoker cat loving dish washer

I am an intrepid ironing laundress
with chronic singer songwriter tendencies
A late-night neighbor wayfarer watercolorist
Seamstress vacation quilt maker, a connector, collector
lover partner whistling trout-fisher
I am a garage-sale salt and pepper shaker soup baker

I am a giver receiver volunteer
picnicking *chi-gung* democrat
Peacenik protester flower child herb gardener
A house painter granddaughter orphan child
Russian Polish American survivor citizen.

Mostly,
I am a list maker.

3rd Place, Lea Killian, Mountain View AR

I've Noticed

Her lips, full and bursting
like rose-colored storm clouds

Her voice, singing with me
in delicate, cursive script

Her fingertips, midnight-dipped
and tracing laugh lines in the sky

Her eyes, autumn-rich and searching
for meaning and melody

—And finally, her love:
a flower unfolding in dark rooms

wondering why it hurts to bloom.

1st Place, Barbara Blanks, Garland TX

Show and Tell

You have got to show me.
    –Congressman Willard Duncan Vandiver

Show me a river that runs through the state
that's mighty, that's muddy, that's wide, and it's long.

Show me a bluebird, the symbol of joy—
no wonder our state is the subject of song.

Show me a dogwood in flowering flaunt—
an all-season wonder in vibrant display.

Show me a honeybee gathering nectar—
gardeners serve them a blossom buffet.

Show me a mule for its sure-footed gait.
It's curious, hard-working, stubborn, and smart.

Show me a hawthorn, a symbol of love.
Though thorny, its blossoms are good for the heart.

Show me Missouri—I'll show you the best—
a fun-loving, friendly, and straight-shooting state.

Show me Missouri—I'll show you a place
with people the reason for making it great.

2nd Place, Grace Diane Jessen, Glenwood UT

Hearing Is Not Enough

Show me the town on the river
where Twain wrote his memorable classics,
the gaslight flat where Joplin, King
of Ragtime, composed entertaining tunes,
the college where Churchill gave a speech
that sparked the start of the cold war.

Show me the parking garage that is built
like a gigantic bookshelf, the monument
where General Grant received his commission,
the street that Walt Disney used as a model
for Disneyland's Main Street, USA.

Show me the Amoureaux House built of logs
set vertically in the earth, the London church
designed by Wren now relocated and restored,
the pony express museum honoring brave riders
who carried the mail two thousand miles west.

Show me some of the six thousand caves
where visitors can take a kayak tour or watch
a black light show or see petrified seaweed,
massive caverns, formations, and bear beds.
Show me where Spanish treasure is believed
to be hidden, the area of the lost copper mine,
the rocks where Bolin and his gang hid out.

Show me the Zombi Road in Wildwood,
Potosi, most haunted town, the shadow folk,
and the ghostly bride under the bridge.
Show me Wilson's Creek battlefield, the view

of Ozark Mountains from Elephant Rocks,
the mysterious stone castle ruins on a bluff.

Show me wildflowers in the tallgrass prairie,
a herd of bison, the trail where my ancestors
left bloody footprints in the snow.
Show me the valley where the Ancient of Days
poke to his posterity, a place for gathering.
Some day, I want to visit and see it all.

3rd Place, Sara Gipson, Scott AR

Show Me Missouri

Show me that place where I can
find a gateway arch that rises
to kiss clouds and beckons
all to visit a state with crowds
steaming to watch pro-sports,
with crowds gathering to hear
famed musicians like ants march
to attack a source of sugar.
Show me where explorers set
points to guide future pioneers
while mapping Louisiana Purchase.
Show me where early settlers
found locations to begin again
and write new chapters of history,
where the Boone brothers built
a mill that launched a town.
Show me where trains of covered
wagons leaped to begin treks west.
Show me a state where fertile farms
grow grass as green as pine boughs.
Show me where rounded hills meet
the Ozark Mountains glowing
like jewels in autumn sunlight,
where mountain springs sprout
to feed hungry streams and rivers
eager to join the mighty Mississippi.
Show me where Samuel Clemens
piloted a river boat and gained
inspiration for literary characters
that still populate imaginations.
Show me a state where dreams
seek reality and families bloom.
Show me the state of Missouri!

1st Place, Martha H. Balph, Millville UT

Stradivarius

The maestro
touches bow
to violin,
ignites the spirit
within.

Seared by awe,
I listen
to what wood
has always
known
about fire.

2nd Place, Beth Ayers, McKinney TX

The Bouquet Taped to the Street Light

The brightly colored bouquet
marked the spot, probably left here
by someone who loved the lost,
someone whose grief was momentarily
managed by the placing of flowers
where a last breath was taken.

Passing here, almost daily, I have seen the
transition of fading colors, shriveled blooms,
still an effective image of grief.
The dried, brown bouquet—
a more poignant reminder of
exactly what happened   here.

3rd Place, Karen Kay Bailey, Blanchard OK

Russian Invasion of Ukraine, 2022

In my kitchen,
Kneading the soft dough of my daily bread,
I am, of a sudden, chilled to the bone—
Shuddering in horror and disbelief at images
Of desperate refugees driven by devastation and fear,
Caught in the wide lens of war.

She has no kitchen now,
She'll take no warm bread from her oven today.
She too, is chilled as she hastens on in wintry weather—
Driven by hope that manna will fall with the dew
Of another anxious, nameless day.

1st Place, Barbara Blanks, Garland TX

Hot Air

We humans are a chatty race.
It's what we do—just yack yack yack.
It's like our words are bric-a-brac
that occupy our time and space.

We babble nonsense, fill each trace
of silence—we don't miss the lack.
We humans are a chatty race—
it's what we do—just yack yack yack.

And at each final resting place
we eulogize—we have the knack.
We never cut ourselves some slack.
It seems that's always been the case.
We humans are a chatty race.

2nd Place, Jerri Hardesty, Bierfield AL

When Comets Fall

When comets fall we watch the skies
And scan the dark with eager eyes
To see those brilliant points of light
That streak across the map of night
Till each one sputters out and dies.

In ancient times, they'd analyze
The meaning, try to realize
The message hidden in the sight
When comets fall.

But now we know the hows and whys,
No longer do we prophesize
On blazing chunks of rock so bright,
We simply gaze with sheer delight
At shooting stars that mesmerize
When comets fall.

3rd Place, Nancy Breen, Loveland OH

The Phantom Children of Morrow Inn

Some people say ghost children play
along the garden walk by day.
Their giggles echo high and sweet
as they rush up as if to greet
a startled guest, then fade away.

Inside at night, they disobey
their former bedtime rules to stray
from attic room to master suite,
some people say.

The guests who witness this display
are often too disturbed to stay.
The sounds of pitter-patter feet
race up the stairs, and then retreat
with yelps and whimpers of dismay,
some people say.

1st Place, Cade Huie, Grand Prairie TX

Tears of Sea

These days a sense of finality hangs,
broods heavy like a pall of smoke
over a charred forest, weaves
its venomous yarn over and through
chipped sky and blackened limb,
binds, chokes, tightens its knots,
forms a timeless suspension
like the pregnant pause before a storm,
when I strain against the restless pressure
of knowing, the foreboding of imminent breakage.
Limbo's question repeats like a monotonous
blow—when will it come?
Yet already the end follows close on our steps,
flooding into our tracks with slow insistence,
grim persistence, this insidious toxicity
of our bastard offspring, for yea, we have salted
our own and only fields, scattered what remains
with the flightless bodies of bees
and poisoned seeds that will never sprout.
We have given our living water
to the Sun in a devil's tribute, have delivered
the gentle days of our youth into the tornado's
greedy hands and the mouth of his hurricane sister
who howls as she feeds on the rising sea.
Yet, we blow the springtime dandelion fluff
with a child's laughing breath, watching it float
high on warming winds, soaring far from our
once fertile Earth, lifting like a flock of distant birds
into the fire, as we turn our backs
on the burning seeds, feigning innocence.
We believe our tears will quench the flames—
our wondrous, magical tears—our tears of regret
that beg forgiveness, our salt ocean tears

that will somehow wash life back
into the browning green of a dying world,
will appease whatever gods remain
to grant new chances for redemption,
to ignore our arson, wash our hands of blame,
allow a few of us to survive, perching like
narcissistic vultures on melting heaps of the dead.

2nd Place, Robert Schinzel, Argyle TX

Crops

It...does not seem to us like Eden promised.
Yes, this dirt...we trample it nightly and daily.
   –Anna Akhmatova, *Our Native Earth*

Wilted leaves
hunch their shoulders
toward earth in endless thirst,
bend as if gravity tugs harder
on plants under stress.
Stunted stems shudder
in gusts of hot wind,
salvation elusive
even as clouds draw near.
Hope ignites and dies
with each flash of dry lightning,
drought standing watch
like a sentinel
sending rain elsewhere.

I dread the prospect of hauling water
from an ever-shrinking creek
a quarter mile from my garden
to irrigate desiccated crops. My back
slumps in fatigue, hunches in futility
from the task ahead,
tongue tracing cracked lips
too blistered to form words,
too dry to utter prayers
lodged in a parched throat.
I grasp two bucket handles
as if they're the hands of my children
and begin the long trek for survival.

3rd Place, Marilyn LT Klimcho, Reading PA

Weather

I have walked in forests,
Listening to their secret talk of weather.
Weather will always be important to the trees.
The woodcutter comes. The woodcutter goes.
He is unimportant. A woodcutter claims
Only the tribute demanded by Caesar.
It is the rising of the sun and the pelting
Of the rain. The gusting of the wind, the weight
Of the snow, and the bitterness of
The temperature. Will the weakest branch
Hold? Or have the carpenter ants finally
Bored a hole too deeply for the branch
To withstand the strain of gravity?
Are the warm southern winds today a fluke,
Or is the back of winter truly broken?
These trees are not gamblers, though
Everything is gambled. They are like the gruff
Old farmers of my grandfather's time,
Who found the weather more important
Than subsequent generations' focus
Upon soccer scores. They are silent, dark,
With everything on the line.
Do the trees of Europe remember
The advance of the last ice age and how
All of them were force marched south?
It was their World War II. Then the talk of trees
Was about terrain and refuge atop the few peaks
Still visible above the mile-deep ice.
In North America the mountain chains ran
North to south. It was easier to flee before
The advancing glacier. Not so easy in Europe
Where the mountains run east to west,

And anyone marched south must meet
The impenetrable walls of the Alps or Pyrenees.
As I walk, the uneasy talk of weather whispers
Overhead, and as among aspens, the news
Travels throughout the rooted upright world
Of trees as they prepare for bad weather.

1st Place, Janet Kamnikar, Fort Collins CO

This Morning

Until the sunrise seeped.in around the bedroom shades,
    I wandered through dreams.
Until I sat up and felt all the old, unfriendly aches returning,
    I was comfortable.
Until I stiff-and-slow-walked to the kitchen,
    I wasn't sure I could move.
Until the coffee made its slow way down
into the pot, then to my cup and down my throat,
    I was barely present.
Until I brought the papers in,
    I thought only of my day and the small
    efforts I would have to make.
Until I turned on the computer,
    I lived in a world the size of one small house.
But then you came down the hall and into the kitchen,
    and I stopped practicing being alone.

2nd Place, Nancy LaChance, Lebanon MO

Cleaning Out the Refrigerator

Why do we have four jars of pickled beets,
two jars of plum jam taking up space,
along with a jar of dill pickle juice
no pickles,
two cellophane bags of lettuce
rotting in the crisper drawer,
last week's leftovers growing green fuzz,
the brick of cheese and whole milk
have expiration dates long overdue,
as do the cold cuts bought at the deli
one month ago?

Being at the hospital took up most
of my time, until she died quietly
in her sleep just a few hours ago.

*I must make room for the funeral food
carried in by neighbors and friends.*

3rd Place, Jenna Pashley, Richmond TX

Collector

She collects odd ducks and taxidermy,
glass eyes set wrongways, squirrely
tails cocked at unusual angles,
art that watches you back.

She collects stories;
you could be in one. Watch yourself.
When she reels you in, you'll lose
an afternoon or more
following the tendrils and trails
of a new set of breadcrumbs.

She collects wanderers.
She'll bring you back
to her cottage in the woods
tell you it's time to fix lunch
that whatever we need is all around us.

She collects knowledge, can conjure
things from the ground
morels, ramps, twisted fiddleheads.
She'll send you home
with feathers in your pockets and
smoke on your skin.

She'll make you a collector too,
though what you lose or gain
in that exchange will be invisible
to the naked eye. You will carry it
under your skin, feel its constant presence
like a weight, an itch unending.

1st Place, Michael Spears, Plain City UT

Bread Day Helpers

Winnie and Ginney, my precious twin girls,
with impish smiles and long blond curls;
I cherished the day that lay ahead,
our weekly hours for baking bread.
  Four little hands helping so,
    kneading and rolling out the dough.
I hummed to myself while I thought of the fray,
as baking with twins takes most of the day.

Oversized aprons faded green,
flour to spare—oh, what a scene!
The kitchen filled with smells so sweet
and joy, with laughter mixed complete.
I smiled to myself while watching the sight,
as baking with twins can be a fright.

With dough on their faces, aprons and table,
I heated the oven and hoped to be able
to bake eight loaves and clean up the mess
from four helping hands, more, or less.
I sighed to myself while viewing the room,
as cleaning with twins takes more than a broom.

The bread raised near the old stove's heat,
as two little twins, whose hands and feet
played with jacks and pick-up sticks,
with London Bridges in the mix.
  Four little hands helping so,
    kneading and rolling out the dough.
I sang to myself while watching bread rise,
as loving play filled my ears and eyes.

Winnie and Ginny are long since grown,
both with grandchildren of their own.
The bread we baked has intertwined
with Eternal Life from the love we mined.
Cuddling two faded aprons my heart has known,
for oh, how the love in my life has grown.
Reminiscing four little hands kneading dough—
Precious marmalade memories from long ago.

2nd Place, Dennis Herschbach, Sartell MN

Birthing Pain
In Memoriam

Last I saw her it was spring.
She was shearing sheep,
guiding clippers over bellies
swollen with unborn lambs.

She stood, stretched her back,
felt new life move within:
under her hand an elbow,
a foot, maybe a knee
pushing for room to grow.
Fingers traced the form
of the unborn child
perfectly shaped, alive.

That spring lambs were born,
white fuzz balls bouncing
here and there, leaping
as newborn lambs do,
cavorting in the pasture
while nervous ewes looked on.

Spring, a time for renewal.
Earth is replenished,
new life unfurls its wonder.
Last I heard, all were born
alive and healthy,
all but one, perfect,
but still.

3rd Place, Susan Chambers, Mankato MN

Legacy for Your Children

You don't know how the tradition started, except
to say that's the way with all traditions, isn't it?
They tiptoe out of something done without intention,
repeated—once, three times. When you neglect it
the next occasion your six-year-old with big eyes looks up,
voice sorrowful, "we always do it this way, it's special."
And there you go—"Muffin Sunday."

So, you creep down in the chill while they still burrow in dreams.
You crack eggs, cream butter and sugar, toss in cinnamon,
raisins or blueberries—whatever the sunrise fancies.
The oven warms you. You inhale the tray out, encourage muffins
with knife and fork onto the yellow plate, trot back up
with a tottering plate full of tangy temptations.

The teapot must come as well, of course, necessitating a second trip.
Now they are awake, tumble into the room, form a circle on the bed:
you prop against the pillows next to father. Son and daughter
are in each corner at your feet, nestled under the fluffy spread.

There is something more at work here than just muffin;
although muffin is crucial to the moment.
And the muffins must be just so: rounded golden peaks,
outer shells a darker brown. The metamorphosis from batter
to muffin is clearly etched over the whole: dense velvet middle,
sweet crust like father's sheltering embrace, top a moon surface,
ridges that liquidly flowed, solidified into peaks during the baking.

We undergo a metamorphosis, too. Our first bite is more than muffin,
dissolved on the tongue. We transform into holy family rituals.
Our custom expands each week. Now there must be a book to go along.

Sundays become golden rings of wizards, arduous journeys, heroic rescues.
Chapters end, leave us dangling over crevices, guarantee a return next Sunday.

Even now, too big to fit under the quilt, they poke adult legs out the sides,
bring a grandson to nestle next to you. They fetch the book,
demand a further chapter, sigh with contentment as the cliff hanger unfolds.
"One more" you say and reach for another muffin.

1st Place, Candy Lish Fowler, St. George UT

Six Observations

I.   A homeless hermit crab…king recycler,
I release him to toss and roll in rising tides
searching for new quarters.

II.   A screeching gull
scoops across crashing surf, flies high,
drops a sea snail (perfect crab house)
onto beach rocks. Gull dives,
digs beak into shattered shell.
In a flurry, the meal is stolen by a flash
of famished feathers.

III.   A sand dollar—
purple, fuzzy, turns my palm yellow.
I cast it back into the churning ocean,
alive.

IV.   An almost perfect circle,
another sand dollar—
white, pristine, sun bleached,
dead. I wash it,
keep it entombed in a pocket
to resurrect later.

V.   A bronze barefoot woman
draped like a bride in ethereal lace,
walks to the cry of mournful bagpipes.
She carries a single rose
and a small carved box to water's edge.

VI.   Ashes…
she sprinkles them over waves.
Wild winds whirl the gray.
Tear-stained cheeks hold the melancholy
of this storm-cast sea.

2nd Place, Daniel Liberthson, Cottage Grove OR

The Lighthouse

We'd a long walk to reach the cove,
rock-hedged under a darkening sky,
you and the part of me
not away on other worlds.
Through anemones and small pine trees
with gulls above as escorts,
we went down, smile and frown,
as the gray air shaped itself between us.

In the lighthouse keeper's cottage
beside the foaming surf
we saw a dolphin rocking horse
on a carpet made of glowing ovals.
A red, red saddle fit its back,
a yellow flower topped its head,
and its green tail was tipped with pink—
no frightful throat, just a cul-de-sac,
safe place to tuck a small, shy fist.

A century plus a decade ago
the lighthouse keeper's little boy
rode this fish with a smiling face,
with its whole body shaped in a smile.
Much faster than a mount with hooves
his swaying, leaping dolphin swam—
skimming an inward, sun-warmed sea
as he shrieked with the pure delight
we too had felt once long ago.

3rd Place, Karen Kay Bailey, Blanchard, OK

Considering Apples by the Sea

On the pier,
The pastry is warm,
The crust is flaky,
    The apples bittersweet—

Moments turn into decades,
Memories rise and fall
Like waves of morning tide
Rushing upon warm sand—
    They linger
    Like the sweetness of blossoms
    Drifting through air.

This place
Is the landmark of yesterdays
For hunters, fishers and sailors of the sea,
For Grandfather—
    The steward
    Of the old apple orchard.

The earth
Holds onto everything
Except the sea—
    The moon will not let it go.

Death
Holds onto everything
Except the memory—
    The heart will not let it go.

1st Place, Maxine B. Kohanski, Tomball TX,

Poor Sadie

Poor Sadie had a problem
of the most unpleasant kind.
The mean old red rooster
would make her lose her mind.

He'd chase her around the yard
then knock her to the ground.
He was the meanest rooster
for miles and miles around.

Sadie couldn't eat or sleep
she always had to hide
her life, a living nightmare,
she refused to go outside.

Her husband said,
"Poor Sadie I'll tell you what I'll do,
I'll kill the mean old rooster,
then your troubles will be through."

Next day she skipped to the barn,
feeling safe and finally free
today there'll be no rooster
to make a fool of me.

Sadie thought she saw a ghost
when she opened up the door
the mean old rooster charged
and knocked her to the floor.

Poor Sadie went half berserk
bitter screams were all they heard.
Her husband made a big mistake
and killed the wrong old bird.

Thrift Store Odyssey

I came here to find a warm wooly hat
to spruce up last year's red winter jacket—
nothing fancy, something black, a beret or cap.
But wait, first I just want to look at that!
It's a scarf, with such beautiful colors
it stands out among all of those others.
But I don't look good in that shade of green
so maybe it's not something I should glean.

Oh! Come over here and look at these jeans.
They even have pink stitching at the seams.
And see how each leg has a lovely rose.
I wonder if they'll fit. Do you suppose?
I'd have to buy a pink blouse to match, then.
Oh now I see someone—has tried to patch them.
So never mind, I'm sure I'll find something better
like maybe this lovely baby blue sweater.
Have you ever seen anything quite so adorable?
But what's this stain? This is just deplorable.

Should I look at the dishes? It would be such fun
to find a charming little green flowered one.
Should I go look at chairs? Don't know where I'd set it.
Or mirrors? Or dressers? Or creme.... I guess I'll forget it.
I've been in here so long, I forgot what I came for.
There's nothing here, I'll just head for the front door.
Well, maybe I'll check out just *one* more rack
What's this? Hooray!
　　　I just found the perfect black hat.

Just Rewards

Womanizer, seducer and rake,
the playboy was known as a snake,
but the ladies still fell for his schemes
since Don Juan was the man of their dreams.

So the women would blush in their tracks,
the flirt used licentious comebacks.
With wanton self-worth he would chase
any female of fair angel face.

Then he would run off with their cash
and spend it with willful panache.
Every day that went by he was sure
there was nothing he couldn't procure.

Houses and yachts, clothing and jewels,
along with a hot blond chanteuse.
Bodyguards, travel, and elegant cars,
they acted like chic superstars.

Rich food everyday, steak and crème brûlée,
plus tickets to plays on Broadway.
It seemed there was never enough,
so he started to play blind man's bluff.

The singer decided to snitch—
her game was—bait-and-switch.
In prison, he now shares a cell
with an inmate who calls him Racquel.

1st Place, Jan Ohmstede, Salida CO

Wildfire

Charcoal bits fall from the dense smoke
obscuring a vermilion sun at high noon.
The stench of torched trees
rides the wind like a harbinger
headed my way.

Chainsaws screech the panic of neighbors
clearing trees around their homes.
Twenty miles beyond, the wildfire advances,
crowning from spruce top to spruce top,
embers igniting the underbrush and alders,
creating its own microclimate.

Only drenching rain or a change
in wind direction will stall it now.
I survey my southwest slope:
towering spruce, birch and aspen bordered
by hundreds of acres of old growth forest.
If fire reaches that north face of black spruce,
high-octane fuel, I will be forced to evacuate.

Images of lifeless, blackened
boreal habitat invade my mind.
I listen.
I smell.
I wait.
Wind gusts strike my face.

2nd Place, Cheryl Van Beek, Wesley Chapel FL

Backdraft

The geography of actual burning depends on the
capacity of the landscape to carry the flames.
        –Stephen J. Pyne, "The human geography
        of fire," *Progress in Human Geography*

My face presses against the scent of old pine.
The doorknob singes my fingers.
Eyelashes spider the keyhole.
Smoke balloons on the other side.
Is it the smoldering past, trapped in my eyes
burning through yesterdays like a diary ablaze?

What's on the other side—
the fog of a confused future rasping
in my throat, that curls under the door
like a cat's gray tail?
My fingers worry a skeleton key.
Sunlight burns through haze, breaks the seal.
The door bursts
open.

3rd Place, Nancy Cook, St. Paul MN

Like No Other Season

Night dresses in Dawn's colors.
This heat is orange. Inescapable.
Aspens don't move a muscle.
Mountain laurels hold their breath.
In the meadow, turkeys raise
a clatter but make no sound,
muffled by the fire's drumbeat.

Shadows of light-hoofed deer
clear the boundary fence.
In the face of angry winds,
eight hundred villagers flee.
There is but one road out. Only
Hermit Jack stands his ground.
Pistol in hand. He'll die here.

If the end ever comes, cold light
will follow rain. The long nights
of flame and fear will leave behind
on car and truck carcasses, on
scattered stone and remnant
steel, deep drifts of fallen ash.
It will be as snow on the moon.

1st Place, Hannah Giuffria, Paron AR

Living in the Shadows

I was known for nothing.
I hope no one will say
I was at my all time high
They were all wrong, in actuality
I was doing my best.
It wasn't a waste of time.
I didn't do it for the money or praise.
That's how I see it.
I was in the shadows.
No one really knows.
They were all blind.
It wasn't a joke
People thought it couldn't be done
I knew that
It could be possible
I needed to change the world.

(now read lines from bottom to top)

2nd Place, Adelaide Spradling, Little Rock AR

My Muse

I know you don't believe in god, or a greater plan, and I like that.
I like the way you see the world.
I believe in God, and a greater plan, and the afterlife.
I believe our souls will meet again.
Even if I'm wrong, I want to experience everything
this world has to offer.
For those who can't and for those who never got to.
Lives cut short in the pursuit of peace.
My soul has been revitalized.
I appreciate life differently.
I'm going to do what I want,
or more so, what feels right.
I pursue happiness like a drug,
the chemicals rushing straight to my brain.
Intoxicated on the changing of the sky,
never the same twice,
and the air leaving our lungs as we sing our favorite songs.
You healed my eternal soul whilst never believing in its existence.

A Locker's Lament

Count up by two's (560, 562 ...)
horizontally. I'm locker no. 564
in the corner faced toward a poster
saying "*BE FREE*" above a
picture of an astronaut gleaming
while gripping planet-turned
balloons that follow closely
behind. I can't move, but does
the poster know that though?

I can't move or go, can't run with
cotton coats bursting and brimming
with warmth in the snowing, icy
cold. But still, so cold I wait
for the warmth of a student's
calloused hands, for them to peer
at my empty interior meant to
store books and binders of the
sort, to be molded to one's vision
of folded or ripped papers on my
painted metal body. A blue, *bleu*,
azul paint, yet I still find
myself looked over like flyers,
hanging on stairway walls through
masking tape that tapers off,
calling out clubs no one cares to
know. Ignored and unseen.

I am but the mere unused locker
no. 564, forgotten in my corner,
faced toward a blaring red exit
sign. Hopeless in waiting.

My Yiayia

When I was born, she was the first to hold me.
I am her namesake.
Some say I have her likeness—an eidetic image.
When I was 6, she gave me my favorite toy.
When I was 8, she gave me her most cherished item,
a gold pendant given to her by her father.
When I was in 3rd grade, I wrote a poem about us.
I remember us making Greek potatoes together.
I remember her teaching me how to bake.
I remember her caring for my Papou when he was sick.
My Yiayia's little Koukla, I am.
My Yiayia is the best, she always has been and always will be.
How stars illuminate the sky at night,
my Yiayia is a constellation—
she is the Bigger Dipper;
and I, the Little.

2nd Place, Parker Heisterkamp, Council Bluffs IA

The Aftermath

The calm, airy, colorful, wilderness
The ruffling sound of leaves crunching beneath my feet
The little rain puddles glistening from the storm
The squirrels peeking out from the trees
The chirping of a dozen birds
The eagle circling for dead prey
The tents and fire pit abandoned
The branches snapped and dangling
The tire marks on the muddy road
The car flipped and totaled
The deer running to find their herd
The mama bears fighting for their cubs
The sirens heard all over
The foxes watching and listening
A helicopter flies overhead with a light blinking
The sirens cut off
The helicopter leaves with the light off....
The birds stop chirping

3rd Place, Kate Laura Kotta, Mason City IA

United

There is a line between crazy and normal,
There is a line between loneliness and popularity,
There is a line between right and wrong,
There is a line between intelligence and stupidity,
Now I draw that line.
I see hatred, violence, insanity.
I see awfulness and destruction.
And I wonder why a single line separating two sides causes so much anger,
I wonder why people pick a side and devote themselves to living that side,
And I celebrate those people who take that line, the line with all the power,
And erase it.

1st Place, Tanya Wyatt, Albuquerque NM

St. George

St. George lived in a little town,
Untouched by king or law;
And every day the people cried
And bad things St. George saw.

The weeks went by, the months went through
And all monsters were gone
And in the gloom, and by the stream
A light on St. George shone.

Then one day St. George left the town
In search of something bad.
A conflict, or a settlement
To give it all he had.

Then one day St. George found a town
Abandoned and unknown.
Out of a hut a maiden wept,
Yet she was all alone.

St. George talked to the maiden
And she told a woeful tale
About a dragon living
On the other side of Dale.

The princess was a sacrifice
To dragon mean and fat.
And when the dragon ate her
That would be the end of that.

When St. George found the dragon,
He called the dragon back

But to his great astonishment
He'd had a heart attack.

So St. George took to wandering
And none have seen him since.
And just in case you're wondering,
The dragon turned to mince.

2nd Place, Bianca Serao, Ames IA

Life

When you see something that you want to do
And you see your life, but you don't think it is you
Though your life might be upside down
Make a smile out of your frown

3rd Place, Tiffany Zhou, Ames IA

Snowflake

Delicate, sparkly
Whirling, blinding, dancing
They're never the same shape

Adams, Deborah; Waverly TN; #4: HM4

Anderson, Sheri; San Antonio TX; #18: HM6

Arnett, Vicki; Preston MO; #42: HM3

Balph, Martha H.; Millville UT; #49: HM3

Barker, Crystal; North Las Vegas NV; #38: HM4

Barker, Crystal; North Las Vegas NV; #9: HM2

Barnes, Patricia; Wyandotte MI; #10: HM2

Barnes, Patricia; Wyandotte MI; #16: HM2

Barnes, Patricia; Wyandotte MI; #18: HM3

Barnes, Patricia; Wyandotte MI; #24: HM3

Barnes, Patricia; Wyandotte MI; #47: HM4

Barnes, Patricia; Wyandotte MI; #8: HM2

Barney, V. Kimball; Kaysville UT; #15: HM5

Barney, V. Kimball; Kaysville UT; #27: HM1

Barreto-Mathews, Joshua; Los Angeles CA; #16: HM3

Berry, Eleanor; Dallas OR; #16: HM5

Berry, Eleanor; Dallas OR; #21: HM6

Blanks, Barbara; Garland TX; #32: HM3

Blanks, Barbara; Garland TX; #36: HM4

Blanks, Barbara; Garland TX; #46: HM5

Blanks, Barbara; Garland TX; #9: HM1

Bond, David; Del Rio TX; #10: HM5

Bouma, Jana; Madison Lake MN; #4: HM6

Braun, Adrienne; Geneva NY; #32: HM1

Bridge, Sunny; Fort Collins CO; #21: HM4

Brosnan, Jim; Assonet MA; #12: HM5

Brosnan, Jim; Assonet MA; #48: HM6

Brown, Roberta; Royal Oak MI; #3: HM5

Casto, Pamelyn; Granbury TX; #17: HM6

Casto, Pamelyn; Granbury TX; #29: HM3

Casto, Pamelyn; Granbury TX; #30: HM7

Chambers, Susan; Mankato MN; #1: HM4

Chambers, Susan; Mankato MN; #25: HM3

Chambers, Susan; Mankato MN; #4: HM5

Chambers, Susan; Mankato MN; #45: HM3

Chisholm, Alison; Southport UK; #14: HM2

Chisholm, Alison; Southport UK; #20: HM6

Chisholm, Alison; Southport UK; #24: HM1

Chisholm, Alison; Southport UK; #30: HM2

Chisholm, Alison; Southport UK; #33: HM2

Chisholm, Alison; Southport UK; #34: HM2

Chisholm, Alison; Southport UK; #35: HM4

Chisholm, Alison; Southport UK; #9: HM5

Chisholm, Alison; Southport UK; #40: HM5

Chisholm, Alison; Southport UK; #50: HM5

Clausen, Kaden; Ames IA; #53: HM5

Coffey, Elliott; Ames IA; #53: HM4

Cook, Crystie; Sandy UT; #9: HM3

Cook, Meredith R.; Blue Earth MN; #22: HM5

Cook, Meredith R.; Blue Earth MN; #26: HM5

Cook, Meredith R.; Blue Earth MN; #3: HM2

Cook, Meredith R.; Blue Earth MN; #50: HM3

Cook, Nancy; St. Paul MN; #31: HM5

Coppock, John W.; Tuttle OK; #24: HM2

Coppock, John W.; Tuttle OK; #44: HM6

Cotton, Kathy Lohrum; Anna IL; #40: HM2

Cotton, Kathy Lohrum; Anna IL; #44: HM5

Cotton, Kathy Lohrum; Anna IL; #23: HM2

Cotton, Kathy Lohrum; Anna IL; #33: HM1

Cotton, Kathy Lohrum; Anna IL; #34: HM6

Cotton, Kathy Lohrum; Anna IL; #35: HM3

Cummings, Julie; Conifer CO; #32: HM6

Curry, Stephen; Jackson MS; #41: HM1

Daubenspeck, Susan; Corpus Christi TX; #13: HM3

Davis, Arianna; Texarkana AR; #51: HM6

Davis, Robert V.; West Haven UT; #29: HM1

Dembosky, Doris; Westcliffe CO; #7: HM6

DeMelfi, Bridget; Cheyenne WY; #52: HM5

Douglas, Lyla; Baxter IA; #53: HM8

Escoubas, Michael; Bloomington IL; #10: HM6

Feeney, Matthew; Moose Lake MN; #15: HM6

Feeney, Matthew; Moose Lake MN; #48: HM7

Felt, Geraldine C.; Layton UT; #45: HM4

Finnegan, Brenda; Ocean Springs MS; #30: HM1

Firmage, Charles K.; Eloy AZ; #41: HM5

Flaugher, Christina; Rochester MN; #18: HM1

Flaugher, Christina; Rochester MN; #2: HM5

Flaugher, Christina; Rochester MN; #38: HM5

Flaugher, Christina; Rochester MN; #5: HM2

Fonce, Dom; Boardman OH; #35: HM6

Fowler, Candy Lish; St. George UT; #13: HM6

Fowler, Candy Lish; St. George UT; #21: HM2

Fowler, Candy Lish; St. George UT; #32: HM5

Fowler, Candy Lish; St. George UT; #37: HM3

Fowler, Candy Lish; St. George UT; #5: HM4

Fox, Greer L.; Knoxville TN; #33: HM7

Freytag, Janice; Souderton PA; #20: HM4

Freytag, Janice; Souderton PA; #23: HM6

Freytag, Janice; Souderton PA; #34: HM1

Funke, Barbara J.; St. George UT; #23: HM4

Funke, Barbara J.; St. George UT; #27: HM5

Funke, Barbara J.; St. George UT; #30: HM5

Funke, Barbara J.; St. George UT; #8: HM1

Gaberman, David; Farmington Hills MI; #46: HM1

Gipson, Sara; Scott AR; #17: HM2

Gipson, Sara; Scott AR; #33: HM3

Glancy, Diane; Gainesville TX; #13: HM2

Glancy, Diane; Gainesville TX; #42: HM7

Glover, Darlene; South Paris ME; #5: HM6

Gordon, Peter; Orlando FL; #41: HM2

Gordon, Peter; Orlando FL; #22: HM3

Gorrell, Dena R.; Edmond OK; #36: HM7

Gorrell, Dena R.; Edmond OK; #44: HM1

Goschy, Deborah; Eagle Lake MN; #15: HM1

Goschy, Deborah; Eagle Lake MN; #23: HM1

Goschy, Deborah; Eagle Lake MN; #35: HM2

Goschy, Deborah; Eagle Lake MN; #45: HM5

Green, Connie; Lenoir City TN; #23: HM3

Green, Connie; Lenoir City TN; #25: HM5

Green, Connie; Lenoir City TN; #30: HM3

Green, Connie; Lenoir City TN; #6: HM3

Green, Connie; Lenoir City TN; #7: HM4

Griswold, Esther Ann; Ft. Collins CO; #13: HM7

Gunn, Gwen; Guilford CT; #14: HM7

Gunn, Gwen; Guilford CT; #2: HM6

Gunn, Gwen; Guilford CT; #3: HM1

Haaland, Hannah; Polk. City IA; #52: HM6

Haltiner, Maurine; Salt Lake City UT; #12: HM7

Haltiner, Maurine; Salt Lake City UT; #26: HM4

Haltiner, Maurine; Salt Lake City UT; #35: HM1

Hamblen, K.; Baton Rouge LA; #21: HM5

Hammerschick, Mark; NAPLES FL; #38: HM2

Hardesty, Jerri; Brierfield AL; #42: HM1

Hardesty, Jerri; Brierfield AL; #6: HM5

Harvey, Dave; Talent OR; #43: HM4

Hasara, Christopher; Renssalear IN; #31: HM1

Hasara, Christopher; Renssalear IN; #50: HM2

Heiden, Magdalene; Alden IA; #52: HM3

Herschbach, Dennis; Sartell MN; #28: HM1

Huff, Melissa; Champaign IL; #10: HM1

Hughes, Betsy M.; Oakwood OH; #10: HM7

Hughes, Betsy M.; Oakwood OH; #11: HM5

Hughes, Betsy M.; Oakwood OH; #31: HM3

Hughes, Betsy M.; Oakwood OH; #44: HM2

Huie, Cade; Grand Prairie TX; #2: HM3

Hurzeler, Richard P.; Tyler TX; #9: HM7

Irish, Amy; Lakewood CO; #16: HM4

Irish, Amy; Lakewood CO; #30: HM4

Irish, Amy; Lakewood CO; #50: HM6

Irish, Amy; Lakewood CO; #7: HM1

Irish, Amy; Lakewood CO; #8: HM5

Irving, Christine; Denton TX; #21: HM3

Irving, Christine; Denton TX; #29: HM4

Irving, Christine; Denton TX; #46: HM7

Isaac, Donna; Inver Grove Heights MN; #23: HM7

Jeffery, Lorraine; Orem UT; #24: HM5

Jeffery, Lorraine; Orem UT; #27: HM6

Jessen, Grace Diane; Gleenwood UT; #27: HM7

Jessen, Grace Diane; Gleenwood UT; #40: HM6

Johnson, Tresina; Urbandale IA; #53: HM1

Jones, Dr. Emory D.; Iuka MS; #31: HM4

Kamnikar, Janet; Fort Collins CO; #10: HM4

Kamnikar, Janet; Fort Collins CO; #21: HM7

Kamnikar, Janet; Fort Collins CO; #31: HM7

Kamnikar, Janet; Fort Collins CO; #39: HM7

Kamnikar, Janet; Fort Collins CO; #41: HM3

Kamnikar, Janet; Fort Collins CO; #47: HM6

Kawahara, Dawn; Lihue HI; #16: HM6

Kawahara, Dawn; Lihue HI; #2: HM4

Killian, Lea; Mountain View AR; #39: HM2

Kim, Hannah; Ames IA; #53: HM2

Klimcho, Marilyn LT; Reading PA; #1: HM1

Klimcho, Marilyn LT; Reading PA; #12: HM1

Klimcho, Marilyn LT; Reading PA; #19: HM1

Klimcho, Marilyn LT; Reading PA; #26: HM2

Kobar, Shirley; Loveland CO; #14: HM3

Kolp, Laurie; Beaumont TX; #29: HM7

Kolp, Laurie; Beaumont TX; #48: HM1

Kolp, Laurie; Beaumont TX; #6: HM2

Kowszik, Paula Sweeney; Millbury MA; #42: HM5

Kretschmann, Jane; Piqua OH; #39: HM5

Kretschmann, Jane; Piqua OH; #11: HM4

Kretschmann, Jane; Piqua OH; #8: HM4

Krotz, Anita M.; Salt Lake City UT; #1: HM2

Krotz, Anita M.; Salt Lake City UT; #13: HM4

Krotz, Anita M.; Salt Lake City UT; #18: HM4

Krotz, Anita M.; Salt Lake City UT; #36: HM2

Krotz, Anita M.; Salt Lake City UT; #43: HM5

Krotz, Anita M.; Salt Lake City UT; #45: HM1

Krotz, Jack; Ainsworth IA; #52: HM2

Krum, Judy; Sanford FL; #43: HM1

Kucera, Luci; Baxter IA; #52: HM7

Kyler, Inge Logenburg; Eaton Rapids MI; #13: HM1

L'Herisson, Catherine; Garland TX; #5: HM7

La Rocca, Lynda; Salida CO; #13: HM5

La Rocca, Lynda; Salida CO; #19: HM3

La Rocca, Lynda; Salida CO; #22: HM7

La Rocca, Lynda; Salida CO; #33: HM6

La Rocca, Lynda; Salida CO; #36: HM1

LaChance, Nancy; Lebanon MO; #49: HM4

Lancaster, Brady; Alden IA; #52: HM1

Lee, Trina; Oklahoma City OK; #47: HM2

Liberthson, Daniel; Cottage Grove OR; #6: HM1

Limmer, Gracie; Little Rock AR; #51: HM2

Magee, Mary Beth; Poplarville MS; #14: HM6

Magee, Mary Beth; Poplarville MS; #26: HM1

Mahal, Laura; Fort Collins CO; #41: HM7

Mahal, Laura; Fort Collins CO; #25: HM1

Mahan, Budd Powell; Dallas TX; #1: HM5

Mahan, Budd Powell; Dallas TX; #14: HM1

Mahan, Budd Powell; Dallas TX; #18: HM2

Mahan, Budd Powell; Dallas TX; #2: HM1

Mahan, Budd Powell; Dallas TX; #24: HM6

Mahan, Budd Powell; Dallas TX; #3: HM4

Mahan, Budd Powell; Dallas TX; #33: HM4

Mahan, Budd Powell; Dallas TX; #38: HM3

Mahan, Budd Powell; Dallas TX; #43: HM2

Mahan, Budd Powell; Dallas TX; #49: HM1

Mardele, Susan; McKinney TX; #6: HM6

Martin, Julie; Saint Paul MN; #34: HM7

Martin, Julie; Saint Paul MN; #37: HM5

Maxwell, Montana; North Little Rock AR; #51: HM4

McCarthy, LaVern Spencer; Blair OK; #15: HM2

McCarthy, LaVern Spencer; Blair OK; #34: HM4

McCarthy, LaVern Spencer; Blair OK; #39: HM1

McDowell, Joy; Springfield OR; #20: HM5

McDowell, Joy; Springfield OR; #29: HM5

McGarry, Sandra; Fort Collins CO; #27: HM2

McGarry, Sandra; Fort Collins CO; #43: HM6

Merrill, Owen; Ames IA; #53: HM6

Miceli, Mary; Rowley MA; #15: HM3

Michaels, Kenneth; York PA; #28: HM7

Miller, Terry; Richmond TX; #50: HM1

Minton, Christopher; Gahanna OH; #28: HM4

Monahan, Amy; West Des Moines IA; #51: HM5

Moore, Sheila Tingley; San Antonio TX; #38: HM6

Moran, Catherine; Little Rock AR; #17: HM4

Moran, Catherine; Little Rock AR; #25: HM7

Moran, Catherine; Little Rock AR; #40: HM7

Moran, Catherine; Little Rock AR; #5: HM5

Morris, Karen; Huntsville AL; #28: HM3

Morris, Karen; Huntsville AL; #6: HM7

Mortenson, Virginia; Des Moines IA; #14: HM4

Mortenson, Virginia; Des Moines IA; #44:

Mounsey, Pauline; Sun City West AZ; #22: HM1

Mounsey, Pauline; Sun City West AZ; #40: HM4

Murthy, Meenakshi; Irving TX; #53: HM7

Mwamba, Gracia; San Lorenzo CA; #4: HM7

Neely, Charlene; Lincoln NE; #8: HM3

Neff, Diane; Oviedo FL; #17: HM7

Neff, Diane; Oviedo FL; #28: HM5

Neff, Diane; Oviedo FL; #36: HM3

Neiswender, James D.; Denton TX; #39: HM3

Neiswender, James D.; Denton TX; #48: HM4

O'Brien, Patricia H.; Old Saybrook CT; #6: HM4

Ohmstede, Jan; Salida CO; #49: HM7

Opsahl, Polly; Oscoda MI; #3: HM7

Opsahl, Polly; Oscoda MI; #43: HM7

Orvis, Mary Ellen; Sun City Center FL; #17: HM1

Orvis, Mary Ellen; Sun City Center FL; #38: HM7

Owens, Michael; Cypress TX; #46: HM6

Panowitsch, Henry; Mankato MN; #17: HM5

Pashley, Jenna; Richmond TX; #41: HM6

Patton, Dennis R.; Alexander AR; #25: HM2

Patton, Dennis R.; Alexander AR; #26: HM6

Patton, Dennis R.; Alexander AR; #37: HM4

Payne, Linda R.; Fairfield OH; #36: HM6

Person, Elaine; Orlando FL; #15: HM7

Person, Elaine; Orlando FL; #2: HM2

Person, Elaine; Orlando FL; #22: HM4

Pories, Mary Jane; Grand Rapids MI; #49: HM5

Quist, William; Minneapolis MN; #32: HM4

Ramos, Dianna; Little Rock AR; #51: HM7

Reid, Erica; Fort Collins CO; #4: HM3

Reisens, Ana; Sant Just Desvern ES; #18: HM7

Reiss-Volin, Linda; Denver CO; #24: HM4

Rodley, Laura; Shelburne Falls MA; #46: HM3

Rogers-Grantham, Mary; Palm Coast FL; #46: HM2

Rogers-Grantham, Mary; Palm Coast FL; #29: HM6

Romano Licht, Lisa; Congers NY; #31: HM2

Rowley, Jo-Anne; Lafayette CO; #37: HM1

Ruth, Janet; Corrales NM; #40: HM1

Ruth, Janet; Corrales NM; #48: HM3

Sacco, Tina; Orlando FL; #1: HM7

Sacco, Tina; Orlando FL; #43: HM3

Salinas, Lisa Toth; Spring TX; #11: HM1

Salinas, Lisa Toth; Spring TX; #16: HM7

Salinas, Lisa Toth; Spring TX; #47: HM1

Santer, Rikki; Columbus OH; #11: HM2

Santer, Rikki; Columbus OH; #7: HM7

Schares, Rose; Ames IA; #53: HM3

Schiffhorst, Lynn; Winter Park FL; #1: HM6

Schiffhorst, Lynn; Winter Park FL; #26: HM3

Schiffhorst, Lynn; Winter Park FL; #35: HM5

Schinzel, Robert; Argyle TX; #21: HM1

Schinzel, Robert; Argyle TX; #22: HM6

Schinzel, Robert; Argyle TX; #44: HM4

Schorr, Veronica; Sherman CT; #25: HM4

Schumann, Aidan; Polk. City IA; #52: HM4

Schwartz, Randy K.; Ann Arbor MI; #20: HM2

Schwartz, Randy K.; Ann Arbor MI; #29: HM2

Schwei, Stephen; Houston TX; #42: HM2

Schwei, Stephen; Houston TX; #46: HM4

Scully, Carolynn J.; Apopka FL; #8: HM6

Sebba, Jon; Murray UT; #2: HM7

Shavin, Julie Kim; Fountain CO; #26: HM7

Shavin, Julie Kim; Fountain CO; #44: HM3

Shea, Pegi; Vernon Rockville CT; #16: HM1

Shiver, Joyce; Crystal River FL; #40: HM3

Shiver, Joyce; Crystal River FL; #49: HM6

Shiver, Joyce; Crystal River FL; #9: HM6

Shute, Christian; Cheyenne WY; #50: HM7

Simmonds, Nancy; Fort Wayne IN; #12: HM4

Simmonds, Nancy; Fort Wayne IN; #3: HM3

Simmonds, Nancy; Fort Wayne IN; #4: HM1

Sims, Wesley; Oak Ridge TN; #20: HM7

Sims, Wesley; Oak Ridge TN; #48: HM5

Spears, Michael; Plain City UT; #12: HM2

Spears, Michael; Plain City UT; #23: HM5

Spears, Michael; Plain City UT; #37: HM7

Stanko, Mary Rudbeck; London Ontario; #17: HM3

Stanko, Mary Rudbeck; London Ontario; #19: HM4

Stanko, Mary Rudbeck; London Ontario; #45: HM6

Stone, Harvey; Johnson City TN; #19: HM5

Stone, Harvey; Johnson City TN; #5: HM1

Stork, Ava; Ankeny IA; #51: HM3

Strauss, Russell; Memphis TN; #18: HM5

Strauss, Russell; Memphis TN; #19: HM6

Strauss, Russell; Memphis TN; #24: HM7

Strauss, Russell; Memphis TN; #31: HM6

Strauss, Russell; Memphis TN; #32: HM2

Strauss, Russell; Memphis TN; #7: HM2

Sweet, Nick; Shepherd TX; #25: HM6

Szarek, Valerie; Louisville CO; #1: HM3

Terry, Mark; Orlando FL; #36: HM5

Terry, Mark; Orlando FL; #45: HM7

Terry, Mark; Orlando FL; #22: HM2

Terry, Mark; Orlando FL; #3: HM6

Terry, Mark; Orlando FL; #38: HM1

Trigg, Laura; Little Rock AR; #47: HM5

Tullis, Judith; LaGrange IL; #20: HM3

Tullis, Judith; LaGrange IL; #47: HM3

Tyner, Janet; Tyler TX; #35: HM7

Underwood, Pat; Colfax IA; #11: HM3

Underwood, Pat; Colfax IA; #42: HM4

Van Beek, Cheryl; Wesley Chapel FL; #45: HM2

Van Beek, Cheryl; Wesley Chapel FL; #10: HM3

Van Beek, Cheryl; Wesley Chapel FL; #19: HM7

Van Beek, Cheryl; Wesley Chapel FL; #47: HM7

Van Beek, Cheryl; Wesley Chapel FL; #7: HM3

Vevang, Curt; Palatine IL; #28: HM2

Vevang, Curt; Palatine IL; #9: HM4

Visser, Wendy; Cambridge, Ontario CA; #32: HM7

Wahl, Mike; Athens AL; #49: HM2

Wahl, Mike; Athens AL; #7: HM5

Walters, S. Evan; Lebanon IN; #14: HM5

Walters, S. Evan; Lebanon IN; #15: HM4

Walters, S. Evan; Lebanon IN; #20: HM1

Walters, S. Evan; Lebanon IN; #42: HM6

Walters, S. Evan; Lebanon IN; #50: HM4

Watson, Janet; Wesley Chapel FL; #33: HM5

Watson, Janet; Wesley Chapel FL; #5: HM3

Whitney, BettyAnn; Wesley Chapel FL; #11: HM7

Whitney, BettyAnn; Wesley Chapel FL; #27: HM4

Wilke, Vicki; Clarkston MI; #34: HM3

Willert, Jeanette; Pell City AL; #30: HM6

Willert, Jeanette; Pell City AL; #48: HM2

Willert, Jeanette; Pell City AL; #8: HM7

Williams, Carol Clark; York PA; #19: HM2

Wilson, Mike; Lexington KY; #12: HM6

Wilson, Mike; Lexington KY; #28: HM6

Wilson, Mike; Lexington KY; #39: HM4

Wilson, Mike; Lexington KY; #4: HM2

Wilson, Mike; Lexington KY; #41: HM4

Wolfe, Lorrie; Windsor CO; #11: HM6

Wolfe, Lorrie; Windsor CO; #12: HM3

Wolfe, Lorrie; Windsor CO; #27: HM3

Wolfe, Lorrie; Windsor CO; #34: HM5

Wolfe, Lorrie; Windsor CO; #37: HM2

Wolfe, Lorrie; Windsor CO; #39: HM6

Zhang, Donna; Rye NY; #51: HM1

Zimmerman, Elaine; Hamden CT; #37: HM6

1. NFSPS Founders Award . . . . Kathleen Cain, Arvada CO

2. The Margo Award . . . . Shirley Blackwell, Los Lunas NM

3. Donald Stodghill Memorial Award . . . . Alan Perry, Marana AZ

4. NFSPS Board Award . . . . Amy Iris, Lakewood CO

5. Winners' Circle Award . . . . Russell Strauss, Memphis TN

6. Georgia Poetry Society Award . . . . Jessica Temple, Fort Walton Beach FL

7. Stone Gathering Award . . . . Mark Andrew Terry, Maitland FL

8. Poetry Society of Texas Award . . . . Mary Schmidt, St. Paul MN

9. Jim Barton, Bard of the Pines Award . . . . Connie Jordan Green, Lenoir City TN

10. Lucille Morgan Wilson Memorial Award . . . . Polly Opsahl, Lake Orion MI

11. Al Laster Memorial Award . . . . Dawn Sly-Terpstra, Lynnville IA

12. Arizona State Poetry Society Award . . . . Jeanette Willert, Pell City AL

13. Jim Barton Memorial Award . . . . Kate Carney (Landow), Denver CO

14. Alabama State Poetry Society . . . . Tilli Urban, Denver CO

15. Land of Enchantment Award . . . . Sally Ortiz, Denver CO

16. Poet's Work Award . . . . Charmaine Pappas Donovan, Brainderd MN

17. The Listening Poem Award . . . . Marleine Yanish, Denver CO

18. Power of Women Award . . . . June Allyn Johnson, Norwalk IA

19. Virginia Corrie-Cozart Memorial Award . . . . Val Szarek, Louisville, CO

20. Mildred Vorpahl Baass Remembrance Award . . . . John Coppock, Tuttle OK

21. League of Minnesota Poets Award . . . . Emily Strauss, Kalamath Falls PA

22. Jessica C. Saunders Memorial Award . . . . Steven Concert, Harvey's Lake PA

23. Poetry Society of Indiana . . . . Alida Rol, Eugene OR

24. Nevada Poetry Society Award . . . . Susan Chambers, Mankato MN

25. William Stafford Memorial Award . . . . Frank Iosue, Oro Valley AZ

26. The New York Poetry Forum Award . . . . Sharon Fox Sweeney, Knoxville TN

27. Columbine Poets of Colorado Award . . . . Eleanor Berry, Dallas TX

28. Morton D. Prouty & Elsie S. Prouty Memorial . . . . Joseph Cavanaugh, Ormond Beach FL

29. Louisiana State Poetry Society Award. . . . . Karen Kay Bailey, Blanchard OK

30. J. Paul Holcomb Memorial Award . . . . Sue Brannan Walker, Mobile AL

31. Utah State Poetry Society Award . . . . Julianza Shavin, Fountain CO

32. Illinois State Poetry Society Award . . . . Budd Powell Mahan, Dallas TX

33. The Robbie Award . . . . Julie Cummings, Conifer CO

34. Iowa Poetry Association Award . . . . Susan Gundlach, Evanston IL

35. Ohio Award . . . . .Jennifer Horne, Cottondale AL

36. Wallace Stevens Memorial Award. . . . . Rita Aiken Moritz, Pell City AL

37. Wyopoets Award . . . . .Jon Sebba, Murray UT

38. Florida State Poets Association, Inc. Award. Barbara Blanks, Garland TX

39. Barbara Stevens Memorial Award . . . . William "Bucky" Ignatius, Cincinnati OH

40. Alice Makenzie Swaim Memorial Award . . . . Nancy Susanna Breen, Loveland OH

41. Jesse Stuart Memorial Award . . . . Lisa Fosmo, Escanaba MI

42. Missouri State Poetry Society Award . . . . .Terrie Jacks, Ballwin MO

43. Massachusetts State Poetry Society Award. . . . . .Louise Brown, Westminster, CO

44. Poetry Society of Oklahoma Award . . . . Florence Bruce, Memphis TN

45. Save Our Earth Award. . . . . .Lori Goetz, Germantown TN

46. Massachusetts State Poetry Society Award. Lorrie Wolfe, Windsor CO

47. Poetry Society of Tennessee Award . . . . Jerri Hardesty, Brierfield AL

48. Maine Poets Society Award. . . . . .Paul Ford, Sandy UT

49. Miriam S. Strauss Memorial Award . . . . Sandra Nantais, Arcadia LA

50. The Poets Northwest Award . . . . .Christina M. Flaugher, Rochester, MN

51. Student Award (Grades 9–12) . . . . .Susan Glassmeyer, Cincinnati OH

52. Poetry In The Classroom (Grades 6–8). . . . . Julia L. George, Muskegon MI

53. Poetry In the Classroom (Grades 3–5) . . . . Julia L. George, Muskegon MI

EXECUTIVE BOARD

President: .... Paul Ford UT

1st Vice President: Development Chair; BlackBerryPeach Prizes for Poetry Chair .... Joseph Cavanaugh FL

2nd Vice President: Contest Sponsors /Brochure Chair .... Steven Concert PA

3rd Vice President: Special Awards Chair .... JoAn Howerton TN

4th Vice President: College Undergraduate Poetry Competition Chair .... Jessica Temple AL

Chancellor ....

1st Vice Chancellor: Stevens Poetry Manuscript Competition Co-chair .... Terry Jude Miller TX

2nd Vice Chancellor: Learning Coordinator .... Peter Stein MN

Secretary: Manningham Trust Competition Chair .... Polly Opsahl MI

Treasurer .... Linda Harris IA

Immediate Past President, Presidential Advisors Chair, Electronic Media, *Strophes* Editor,

Contest Chair, Electronics Media Assistant .... Julie Cummings CO

APPOINTIVE BOARD

Board Liaison to State Societies, Membership Chair .... Russell H. Strauss TN

Convention Coordinator .... Susan Stevens Chambers MN

Encore Prize Poems Editor .... Kathy Lohrum Cotton IL

Historian .... Nancy Baass TX

Judges Chair .... Carla Jordon CO

Legal Counselor, Parliamentarian .... Susan Stevens Chambers MN

Librarian .... Catherine L'Herisson TX

Manningham Trust Advisor .... Sam Wood NV

Performance Poetry Advocate ....

Poetry Day, Poetry Month Liaison .... Amy Jo Zook OH

Publicity Chair .... Bernadette Perez NM

Stevens Manuscript Competition Co-Chair .... Eleanor Berry OR

Webmaster .... Billy Pennington OK

Youth Chair .... JC Wayne NM

HONORARY CHANCELLORS

1960 Joseph Auslander
1962 John Crowe Ransom
1963 Glenn Ward Dresbach
1964 Jesse Stuart
1965 Grace Noll Crowell
1966 Jean Starr Untermeyer
1968 Loring Williams
1969 Harry M. Meachum
1970 John Williams Andrews
1971 August Derleth
1972 William E. Stafford
1973 N. Scott Momaday

1974 Richard Armour
1975 Richard Eberhart
1976 James Dickey
1977 Judson Jerome
1979 John Ciardi
1981 Robert Coles
1983 Richard Shelton
1985 Marcia Lee Masters
1986 Robert Penn Warren
1987 Richard Wilber
1990 William E. Stafford
1992 Rodney Jones

1995 Tess Gallagher
1997 Michael Bugeja
2000 David Wagoner
2002 Maxine Kumin
2004 Naomi Shihab Nye
2006 Li Young Lee
2008 Lewis Turco
2010 Ted Kooser
2012 Natasha Trethewey
2015 Peter Meinke
2018 Jo McDougall
2019 David Rothman

NFSPS PRESIDENTS

1959–1960	Cecilia Parsons Miller*	Pennsylvania Poetry Society
1960–1961	Clinton F. Larson*	Utah State Poetry Society
1961–1962	Robert D. West*	Ohio State Poetry Society
1962–1964	Edna Meudt*	Wisconsin Fellowship of Poets
1964–1966	Marvin Davis Winsett*	Poetry Society of Texas
1966–1968	Max C. Golightly*	Utah State Poetry Society
1968–1970	Hans Juergensen*	West Virginia Poetry Society
1970–1972	Russell Ferrall*	Wisconsin Fellowship of Poets
1972–1974	Jean Jenkins*	Utah State Poetry Society
1974–1976	Catherine Case Lubbe*	Poetry Society of Texas
1976–1978	Glenn Robert Swetman	Louisiana State Poetry Society
1978–1979	Carl P. Morton*	Alabama State Poetry Society
1979–1981	Alice Briley*	New Mexico State Poetry Society
1981–1983	Wauneta Hackleman*	Arizona State Poetry Society
1983–1885	Jack E. Murphy*	Poetry Society of Texas
1985–1987	Barbara Stevens*	South Dakota State Poetry Society
1987–1988	Henrietta A. Kroah*	Florida State Poets Association, Inc.
1988–1990	Jerry Robbins*	Kentucky State Poetry Society
1990–1992	Pat Stodghill	Poetry Society of Texas
1992–1994	Wanda B. Blaisdell*	Utah State Poetry Society
1994–1996	Ralph Hammond	Alabama State Poetry Society
1996–1998	Amy Jo Zook	Verse Writers Guild of Ohio
1998–2000	Susan Stevens Chambers	League of Minnesota Poets
2000–2002	Clarence P. Socwell*	Utah State Poetry Society
2002–2004	Madelyn Eastlund	Florida State Poets Association, Inc.
2004–2006	Budd Powell Mahan	Poetry Society of Texas
2006–2008	Doris Stengel	League of Minnesota Poets
2008–2010	Nancy Baass	Poetry Society of Texas
2010–2012	Russell H. Strauss	Poetry Society of Tennessee
2012–2014	Jeremy Downes	Alabama State Poetry Society
2014–2016	Eleanor Berry	Oregon Poetry Association
2016–2018	Jim Barton*	Poets' Roundtable of Arkansas
2018–2022	Julie Cummings	Columbine Poets of Colorado
2022–2024	Paul Ford	Utah State Poetry Society

*Deceased

1. NFSPS Founders Award. Subject: Any. Form: Any. 100 line limit. Sponsored by NFSPS, Inc. 1st Prize: $1,000. 2nd Prize: $500. 3rd Prize: $250.

2. The Margo Award. Subject: Windows. Form: Any. 50 line limit. Sponsored by her friends in memory of Margo LaGattuta. 1st Prize: $200. 2nd Prize: $100. 3rd Prize: $50.

3. Donald Stodghill Memorial Award. Subject: Any. Form: Any. Sponsored by Pat Stodghill. 1st Prize: $200. 2nd Prize: $100. 3rd Prize: $50.

4. NFSPS Board Award. Subject: Any. Form: Golden Shovel. 50 line limit. Sponsored by the NFSPS Executive and Appointive boards. 1st Prize: $170. 2nd Prize: $100. 3rd Prize: $60.

5. Winners' Circle Award. Subject: Any. Form: Any. 80 line limit. Sponsored by Diane Glancy, Pat Stodghill, Sue Chambers (previous Founders Award winners) 1st Prize: $150. 2nd Prize: $80. 3rd Prize: $30.

6. Georgia Poetry Society Award. Subject: The American South. Form: Any. Sponsored by the Georgia Poetry Society. 1st Prize: $150. 2nd Prize: $75. 3rd Prize: $25.

7. Stone Gathering Award. Subject: Food and Food ways. Form: Prose poem. Sponsored by Danielle Dufy Literary French Press Editions. 1st Prize: $125. 2nd Prize: $75. 3rd Prize: $50.

8. Poetry Society of Texas Award. Subject: Any. Form: Any. Sponsored by the Poetry Society of Texas. 1st Prize: $125. 2nd Prize: $50. 3rd Prize: $25.

9. Jim Barton, Bard of the Pines Award. Subject: In the Pines. Form: Rhymed. Sponsored by the South Arkansas Poets of the Pines. 1st Prize: $100. 2nd Prize: $60. 3rd Prize: $40.

10. Lucille Morgan Wilson Memorial Award. Subject: Garden. Form: Any. Sponsored by Julie Cummings and Carla Jordan. 1st Prize: $100. 2nd Prize: $60. 3rd Prize: $40.

11. Al Laster Memorial Award. Subject: An Ekphrastic Poem. Form: Any. 50 line limit. Sponsored by Diana Gagne.1st Prize: $100. 2nd Prize: $50. 3rd Prize: $50.

12. Arizona State Poetry Society Award. Subject: When the door closes. Form: Any. Sponsored by the Arizona State Poetry Society (ASPS).1st Prize: $100. 2nd Prize: $50. 3rd Prize: $25.

13. Jim Barton Memorial Award. Subject: Any. Form: Any. Sponsored by the Poets Roundtable of Arkansas 1st Prize: $75. 2nd Prize: $50. 3rd Prize: $25.

14. Alabama State Poetry Society Award. Subject: Breaking the Rules. Form: Modify an existing form to make it your own. 50 line limit. Sponsored by the Alabama State Poetry Society. 1st Prize: $75. 2nd Prize: $50. 3rd Prize: $25.

15. Land of Enchantment Award. To honor the memory of Susan Paquet Subject: Borders. Form: Any. Sponsored by the New Mexico State Poetry Society. 1st Prize: $75. 2nd Prize: $50. 3rd Prize: $25.

16. Poet's Work Award. Subject: Life as Other. Form: Persona poem. Sponsored by Paul Ford and Marie Andrews. 1st Prize: $75. 2nd Prize: $50. 3rd Prize: $25.

17. The Listening Poem Award. Subject: Listening. Form: Any. Sponsored by Linda Eve Diamond. 1st Prize: $75. 2nd Prize: $50. 3rd Prize: $25.

18. Power of Women Award. Subject: The Power of Women. Form: Any. Sponsored by Sue Chambers and Christina Flaugher. 1st Prize: $70. 2nd Prize: $50. 3rd Prize: $20.

19. The Virginia Corrie-Cozart Memorial Award. Subject: Reflections. Form: Any. Sponsored by her friends in the Peregrine Writers. 1st Prize: $60. 2nd Prize: $40. 3rd Prize: $20.

20. Mildred Vorpahl Baass Remembrance Award. Subject: Domestic Cats . Form: Any. Sponsored by her daughter, Nancy Baass. 1st Prize: $60. 2nd Prize: $40. 3rd Prize: $20.

21. League of Minnesota Poets Award. Subject: Any. Form: Free Verse. 45 Line Limit. Sponsored by the League of Minnesota Poets. 1st Prize: $60. 2nd Prize: $40. 3rd Prize: $20.

22. Jessica C. Saunders Memorial Award. Subject: Any. Form: Villanelle. 19 Line Limit. Sponsored by the Shavano Poets Society of Colorado. 1st Prize: $60. 2nd Prize: $40. 3rd Prize: $20.

23. Poetry Society of Indiana Award. Subject: A Daily Ritual. Form: Any. Sponsored by the Poetry Society of Indiana. 1st Prize: $50. 2nd Prize: $30. 3rd Prize: $20.

24. Nevada Poetry Society Award Subject: Any. Form: Rondino. 32 Line Limit. Sponsored by the Nevada Poetry Society. 1st Prize: $50. 2nd Prize: $30. 3rd Prize: $20.

25. William Stafford Memorial Award. Subject: Any. Form: Any. Sponsored by the Oregon Poetry Association and Friends of William Stafford. 1st Prize: $50. 2nd Prize: $30. 3rd Prize: $20.

26. The New York Poetry Forum Award. Subject: The Art of Poetry. Form: Any. Sponsored by the New York Poetry Forum. 1st Prize: $50. 2nd Prize: $30. 3rd Prize: $20.

27. Columbine Poets of Colorado Award. Subject: Any. Form: Haibun. 30 Line Limit. Sponsored by the Columbine Poets of Colorado.1st Prize: $50. 2nd Prize: $30. 3rd Prize: $20.

28. Morton D. Prouty & Elsie S. Prouty Memorial Award. Subject: Nature poem. Form: Any. Sponsored by daughters, Catherine P. Horn and Carol P. Ostberg and their families. 1st Prize: $50. 2nd Prize: $30. 3rd Prize: $20.

29. Louisiana State Poetry Society Award. Sponsored by the Louisiana State Poetry Society. Subject: Any. Form: Any. 1st Prize: $50. 2nd Prize: $30. 3rd Prize: $20.

30. J. Paul Holcomb Memorial Award. Subject: Any. Form: Any. 28 Line Limit. Sponsored by the Poetry Society of Texas. 1st Prize: $50. 2nd Prize: $30. 3rd Prize: $20.

31. Utah State Poetry Society Award. Subject: Double Vision. Form: Any. 50 Line Limit. Sponsored by the Utah State Poetry Society.1st Prize: $50. 2nd Prize: $30. 3rd Prize: $20.

32. Illinois State Poetry Society Award. Subject: Books. Form: Any. Sponsored by the Illinois State Poetry Society. 1st Prize: $50. 2nd Prize: $30. 3rd Prize: $20.

33. The Robbie Award. Subject: Loss of a Child (not necessarily by death). Form: Any. Sponsored by Joyce Wilson. 1st Prize: $50. 2nd Prize: $30. 3rd Prize: $20.

34. Iowa Poetry Association Award. Subject: Poetry for Children. Form: Any. 50 Line Limit. Sponsored by the Iowa Poetry Association.1st Prize: $50. 2nd Prize: $30. 3rd Prize: $20.

35. Ohio Award. Subject: Any. Form: Any. Sponsored by the Ohio Poetry Association. 1st Prize: $50. 2nd Prize:$25. 3rd Prize: $15.

36. Wallace Stevens Memorial Award. Subject: Any. Form: Rondeau. Sponsored by the Pennsylvania Poetry Society, Inc. 1st Prize: $40. 2nd Prize: $25. 3rd Prize: $15.

37. WyoPoets Award. Subject: Wyoming or the West. Form: Any. Sponsored by the WyoPoets of Wyoming. 1st Prize: $40. 2nd Prize: $25. 3rd Prize: $15.

38. Florida State Poets Association, Inc. Award. Subject: Florida. Form: Any. Sponsored by the Florida State Poets Association, Inc. 1st Prize: $35. 2nd Prize: $25. 3rd Prize: $15.

39. Poetry Society of Michigan Award. Subject: Any. Form: Free Verse. Sponsored by the Poetry Society of Michigan. 1st Prize: $35. 2nd Prize: $25. 3rd Prize: $15.

40. Mississippi Poetry Society Award. Subject: Any. Form: Sonnet. Sponsored by the Mississippi Poetry Society. 1st Prize: $35. 2nd Prize: $25. 3rd Prize: $15.

41. Jesse Stuart Memorial Award. Subject: Any. Form: Any. Sponsored by the Kentucky State Poetry Society. 1st Prize: $25. 2nd Prize: $20. 3rd Prize: $15.

42. Missouri State Poetry Society Award. Subject: The Show Me State. Form: Any. Sponsored by the Missouri State Poetry Society. 1st Prize: $25. 2nd Prize: $20. 3rd Prize: $15.

43. Barbara Stevens Memorial Award. Subject: Any Serious Theme. Form: Any. 12 Line Limit. Sponsored by the South Dakota State Poetry Society. 1st Prize: $25. 2nd Prize: $20. 3rd Prize: $15.

44. Poetry Society of Oklahoma Award. Subject: Any. Form: Rondeau. 13 Line Limit. Sponsored by the Poetry Society of Oklahoma. 1st Prize: $25. 2nd Prize: $20. 3rd Prize: $15.

45. Save Our Earth Award. Subject: Environmental Issues. Form: Any. Sponsored by the Martha H. Balph.1st Prize: $25. 2nd Prize: $20. 3rd Prize: $15.

46. Massachusetts State Poetry Society Award. Subject: Any. Form: Any. Sponsored by the Massachusetts State Poetry Society. 1st Prize: $25. 2nd Prize: $20. 3rd Prize: $15.

47. Poetry Society of Tennessee Award. Subject: Families. Form: Any. Sponsored by the Poetry Society of Tennessee. 1st Prize: $25. 2nd Prize: $20. 3rd Prize: $15.

48. Maine Poets Society Award. Subject: The Sea or Seacoast. Form: Any. Sponsored by the Maine Poets Society. 1st Prize: $25. 2nd Prize: $20. 3rd Prize: $15.

49. Miriam S. Strauss Memorial Award. Subject: Humorous Poem. Form: Rhymed, Metered. 30 line limit. Sponsored by Russell H. Strauss. 1st Prize: $25. 2nd Prize: $20. 3rd Prize: $15.

50. The Poets Northwest Award. Subject: The Geography of Fire. Form: Any. 36 line limit. Sponsored by Poets Northwest, a chapter of the Poetry Society of Texas. 1st Prize: $25. 2nd Prize: $20. 3rd Prize: $15.

STUDENT CONTESTS

51. Student Award: Grades 9–12. Subject: Any. Form: Any. 32 line limit. Sponsored by Julie Cummings and Catherine L'Herisson. 1st Prize: $50.00 . 2nd Prize: $30.00 . 3rd Prize: $20.00. 7 Honorable Mentions: $5.00 each.

52. Poetry in the Classroom Award: Grades 6–8. Subject: Any. Form: Any. 32 line limit. Sponsored by the New Mexico State Poetry Society. 1st Prize: $25.00. 2nd Prize: $15.00. 3rd Prize: $10.00.

53. Poetry in the Classroom Award: Grades 3–5. Subject: Any. Form: Any. Sponsored by the New Mexico State Poetry Society. 1st Prize: $25.00. 2nd Prize: $15.00. 3rd Prize: $10.00

Made in the USA
Columbia, SC
09 August 2022

64905217R00124